Black Fury

To Jan

Merry Xmas

O. Ch

Dec 12/13

Library and Archives Canada Cataloguing in Publication
Miller, Donna, 1951-
Black fury / Donna Miller.

(Help me, I'm naked ; bk. 1)
ISBN 978-1-894431-79-8

I. Title. II. Series: Miller, Donna, 1951- . Help me, I'm naked ; bk. 1.

PS8626.I447B53 2012 C813'.6 C2012-904807-0

FSC
www.fsc.org
MIX
Paper from responsible sources
FSC® C016245

Cover image © Joey Boylan/istockphoto.com
Author photo: Jane Martens
Editing and Design: Heather Nickel

Printed and bound in Canada by Friesens Printers
First printing: August 2012
Second printing: February 2013

Your Nickel's Worth Publishing
Regina, SK.

www.yournickelsworth.com

ENVIRONMENTAL BENEFITS STATEMENT

Your Nickel's Worth Publishing saved the following resources by printing the pages of this book on chlorine free paper made with 100% post-consumer waste.

TREES	WATER	ENERGY	SOLID WASTE	GREENHOUSE GASES
4 FULLY GROWN	1,611 GALLONS	1 MILLION BTUs	102 POUNDS	357 POUNDS

Environmental impact estimates were made using the Environmental Paper Network Paper Calculator. For more information visit www.papercalculator.org.

To the women in my life
and to Mother God

Acknowledgements

I have a story to tell—a true story. To protect the privacy of others, most names have been changed.

For their help in critiquing my book, I would like to thank my daughter, Shauna, and granddaughters, Katharina Russel, Victoria Connell and Amber; my friend, Jane Martins; and the Rosetown Writers Group. I would also like to thank my daughter, Kennalyn—without whose ability to troubleshoot computers this book would never have gone beyond a handwritten copy.

A special thanks to my mother, Katharina, to my children—Katharine, Shauna, Velvet, Kennalyn, Kenny and Kian—to my ten grandchildren, and to Chris Ewing-Weisz, Cindy Cerniuk, Joan Robbie and Helen Mourre, for their faith in my writing. My heartfelt appreciation to Velvet, who insisted I get internet installed, and to my grandson, Henry Russel, who showed me how to use it.

Last but not least, I would like to thank my editor and publisher, Heather Nickel, for her patience and hard work; without her there wouldn't be a book.

Prologue

Something wakes me up. A sound. I listen.

There...again.

What is that noise?

A small figure topped with a halo of moon-coloured hair, I creep out of bed. I open the bedroom door and peer into the living room.

Mommy is on the couch. Daddy is beside her.

I edge closer.

Daddy's got his hands on Mommy's throat. Mommy is making funny noises. *Mommy can't breathe!*

"Daddy! Daddy! You're hurting Mommy!"

Part One

1943 - 1954

1

My mother, Angelina, met Joe during the war years. She was boarding in Saskatoon at a convalescent home where she worked as a nurse's aide.

"It was on a Sunday," Mom told me...

Angelina had the whole day off to do with as she pleased. Though she usually worked Friday through Wednesday, with Thursdays off, that week she had been given a free Sunday as well. This was a rare treat for her since few of her days were ever really hers to enjoy.

On Wednesdays after work she was expected to walk home to the farm, a distance of four miles, so that she could give her mother a hand around the house, and then walk back to the city the evening of the next day. One time she had been so tired that, intending to just sit for a minute in a field, she had fallen asleep instead. Fortunately it had been warm out.

Angelina had begun the day by sleeping late into the

morning, then relaxing in a steamy, luxurious bubblebath. She skipped breakfast but had a long, slow lunch.

Back in her room she reached for a book to read, then changed her mind. It was a sunny afternoon in May, too nice a day to waste indoors. There was an orchestra playing in the park by the Bessborough Hotel.

Angelina decided she would take it in. She put on a blue denim jumper that she and her mother, together, had sewn, and a long sleeved white blouse. She applied rouge to her cheeks, a little colour to her full lips, and a touch of mascara on the lashes framing her lovely hazel eyes.

Waist-length golden tresses flouncing with each step, Angelina strolled toward the park. As she drew nearer, strains of the big band tune “In the Mood” excited her ears. She quickened her pace.

Angelina wove among the throngs of people. Privates in uniform held hands with their dreamy-eyed sweethearts; families from the country dressed in their Sunday best. There were blue-collared workers and white.

Angelina slowly made her way closer to the bandstand. She passed a grizzled old man who flitted here and there collecting discarded pop bottles for which he would receive a penny each at the corner store, and passed a rotund rosy-cheeked grandmother who called out to a small boy, “Don’t wander too close to the river, Johnny!”

Angelina found a spot near the gazebo and sat down. She hadn’t brought a mat to sit on, but the grass, unlike the patches of rough sod back home, was warm and luscious. Her eyes and ears took in the scene. It was truly a gala affair. Blankets were spread out and picnic baskets opened. A toddler in baggy-bottomed pants waddled past, followed by his mother, a pretty, young housewife in a faded gingham dress.

The orchestra was performing "Fraulein" when Angelina noticed someone standing beside her; someone with shoes buffed to a mahogany shine. She looked up to see a man clad in a navy pinstriped suit and necktie and powder blue shirt. He looked to be in his early twenties.

"Excuse me," he asked, "Would you mind if I join you?"

"No, not all." Angelina scooted over to share her patch of grass.

"I'd like to introduce myself." He extended his hand. "Joe Jaslo from New Toronto, Ontario."

Angelina shook his hand. "Pleased to meet you, Joe. I'm Angelina Bickert. What brings you to Saskatoon?"

"I'm an airframe mechanic in the RCAF. I'm presently stationed here."

"Oh," she said somewhat nonplussed. He didn't look like a mechanic. His hands were those of an artist. The fingers were long and slender and the nails clean.

"So what exactly is it that you do?"

Joe ran a hand through his thick dark brown curls. "It's my duty to service the planes they use to train air crew."

"That sounds like a pretty important job."

"Well, yes, it is. It's important the aircraft be kept in top-notch running condition." He switched his attention to her. "So are you from around these parts?"

"Well, I was born in Warman but I've lived in places in and around Saskatoon, Aberdeen, and the Sand Hills area. I'm working at the Saskatoon Convalescent Home, but my family lives on a farm just outside the city."

They continued to chat between songs. Angelina learned that Joe was born in Poland and had one older and two younger brothers, and a sister—the baby of the family. Joe learned that Angelina, the oldest of a family of six, had four sisters and one brother.

Angelina found Joe to be a stimulating, intelligent person. He explained the aerodynamics that enabled a plane to fly. He spoke of the lift, the air thrusting upward on the wings, that supported the weight of the plane.

"When you think of it," he said, "planes—and cars as well—function much like a living body does. The headlights, the tires, the engine and gasoline tank find their counterparts in our eyes, feet, heart and stomach respectively. And like us they need fuel to operate."

As a nurse's assistant, Angelina was engrossed. "I never thought of it that way," she remarked.

In turn, Joe found Angelina's talk of things she had learned at the convalescent home of interest to him. What especially caught his attention was her account of a certain elderly woman who resided there.

"Every morning the lady touches my sleeve. And she always comments on the colour of my blouse, 'Oh you're wearing blue today,' or pink or whatever the colour happens to be. I never thought much of it until one day I was told she is blind. I was shocked—there must have been some mistake, I thought. So I asked the lady and she said that yes indeed she was blind. To prove it, she took out her glass eyes. 'But how is it that you can tell what colour blouse I'm wearing each day?' I asked her. The lady said, 'It's easy. My hands can feel the colour.'"

"I'm not at all surprised," Joe commented. "People can't begin to fathom the ability of the human mind. Do you know that the average person utilizes only a small portion of his brain?"

Time flew as they alternately talked and listened to the music. It was with reluctance a couple of hours later that Angelina announced it was time for her to leave.

When Joe stood and helped her to her feet, he looked

down in surprise. He had figured she was short but not this diminutive. She barely reached the height of his chest; he was five-foot nine.

"May I walk you back to your residence?" he asked.

Angelina, accustomed to farm boys, was impressed with his gentlemanly manners and his meticulous appearance and agreed to allow him to escort her.

As they walked, Joe asked Angelina if she liked to dance.

Liked to dance? Oh, how Angelina *loved* to dance! Her papa had taught her how to tap dance and then how to waltz when she was only three years old. How she missed those happier times, those days before Papa changed.

Angelina's parents were what her mother's side called *Plautdietsch* and what her father's side called Pennsylvania Dutch. They were descendants of a group of people who fled the Netherlands in 1550 due to religious persecution from the Catholic Church. Followers of this faith had become known as Mennonites, pacifists who believed in adult baptism and a simple, hard working lifestyle.

Angelina's maternal grandparents had raised their children in the traditional strict Mennonite way, but Angelina's father's parents were much less austere. They even drank and danced! And so Abe, their son, grew up to be far more liberal than many of his fellow brethren. Nonetheless, or perhaps because of it, Margaretha, Angelina's mother, fell in love with and married him.

A couple of years later, Angelina, their firstborn, came into the world. In Abe Bickert's eyes she was perfect. He said that she had the face of an angel; blond curls surrounding a cherubic face. Though more children soon followed, Abe continued to call Angelina his *kjleenet Kjint*—his little one. He taught her how to dance. They would start out tap-dancing then break into a waltz or a square dance or just some move he made up as they went along. And as Abe led, Angelina followed. How proudly he smiled when visitors came and complimented him on his pretty, petite, talented little girl.

Margaretha would frown and complain. She didn't like such frolicking in her house nor did she especially care for the favouritism her husband bestowed on their eldest.

But Abe would simply say to her, "Don't be so *nechst me'jal.*"

Angelina was six years old the summer Abe went to work for a wealthy pig farmer near the village of Haltein. As was usual when he went to work for a farmer, his family came with him, moving into the house the employer provided. The farmer and his wife were childless and became so enchanted with Angelina that they offered the Bickerts the farm and all that went with it, as well as two thousand dollars cash, for her.

Abe and Margaretha turned the farmer down.

Later, when Margaretha was alone with Abe, she said, "See, have I not told you that the way you are with that girl is sinful? Look, now—people are even wanting to buy her. It's the devil's work. She is turning into a temptress."

Around that same time, Abe was afflicted with a hernia and was told he needed an operation. It was serious. Abe was worried. He had a wife and children to support. What if he could no longer work?

For years Margaretha had been pressuring Abe to reform, to give up his sinful ways of drinking, smoking and dancing and to turn his life to the Lord. Abe now made a deal with God: *Lord, if you let me survive the knife and make it so I can work again, I will give my life to You.*

Abe did live to grow strong again. And he kept his promise. He turned from the pleasures of the world and began attending church, but he changed in other ways as well. Where he used to laugh and joke, he now scowled and scorned. He took the whip to his horses and the belt to his children.

Thinking about it, Angelina sighed. In essence, she had lost her papa. How she missed him.

"Yes," Angelina now answered Joe. "I love to dance!"

"Good. There's music at the Royal Canadian Legion every weekend. How about I pick you up some Friday?"

2

ANGELINA SAW HIM sitting in the visitors' room, as impeccably dressed as before.

Joe stood when he saw her. "I've come to take you dancing tonight," he declared. "What time do you get off?"

"In another hour."

"I'll wait for you."

When her shift ended she quickly changed, slipping on a dress the colour of a prairie sky on a hot summer's day. She applied a little rouge to her already rosy cheeks and put on some lipstick before releasing her thick blond waves from her cap. Just before stepping out she donned a pair of white heels.

I don't even care if he's the type who'll step on my toes. I'm going dancing tonight!

She hadn't gone dancing since the time she had snuck away with her sister Kathy. She and Kathy—a year younger than herself—had occasionally gone out with two brothers, Isaac and Jake, from among their people. They would go for picnics together or sometimes for a drive in Isaac's convertible.

One fall evening, Kathy and Angelina had climbed out the bedroom window to sneak away with the brothers to go to a dance. Though Isaac had stepped on her toes, Angelina hadn't cared. It had been so much fun just to dance again.

THE LEGION WAS three-quarters full and filling fast when Joe signed Angelina in. They barely had time to find a table and order drinks before the music began. From then on the night was a whirlwind of waltzes, foxtrots and polkas. Joe taught her how to jive and do the jitterbug too. And where Joe led, Angelina followed.

Angelina was enchanted. *It's as though we've been dancing together all our lives!*

Joe kissed her that night and vowed he was going to make this pretty little lady who was able to follow his every move his wife.

Joe and Angelina went dancing at the Legion whenever he had a free Friday or Saturday evening, which in Angelina's eyes wasn't nearly often enough. Joe showered Angelina with affection. He held her hand, ran his fingers through her long, soft hair. Once, while waltzing, he whispered to her, "The eyes of every man in this place are on you. Each of them wishing he was holding you." His eyes shone fierce and electric blue, proud to be the lucky one.

They had gone on only a handful of dates when Joe first asked Angelina to marry him.

"But we barely know each other," she replied.

"But look how well we dance together; that shows how in tune with each other we are!"

They had known each other for three months the first

time Joe visited the farm. He was able to get a Thursday off so he surprised her by showing up one morning. Angelina introduced him to her mother as a friend.

Margaretha had been trying to replace a loose step on the porch.

"Here, Mrs. Bickert, let me give you hand," Joe said. He rolled up his sleeves and set to work. Before long he had fixed not only the step but the rickety railing as well.

Hmm, Margaretha thought, *the young man knows how to work. That's unusual for the* Enjelsch. Anyone outside the Bickert's own people was considered one of the English, the "other people."

What Angelina noticed was that when Joe was finished with the repairs, he had not a smudge of grime on his clothes. She was impressed. *Not too many men can work without getting themselves dirty.*

Joe then went on to chop wood for Margaretha and bring in pails of water from the well for her. *My what a helpful boy,* she thought. *And so respectful!* He kept calling her "ma'am."

Suppertime approached. Margaretha told Kathy to set the table for one more. The young man had been so helpful today. She must feed him. Besides, to not invite him to join in the meal would be considered inhospitable—*nijch oppnament.*

"Seat, seat," she said to Joe, motioning to the table.

It was a simple meal—fried potatoes and roast pork with watermelon pickles, and cucumber and cream salad—but it was filling.

Angelina's sisters were enchanted by her handsome, charismatic friend. He joked with them and regaled them with stories.

"I built my first short-wave radio when I was only ten

years old," he said, "And the police couldn't figure out where the interference was coming from."

Oh but, my, how smart he is, they thought.

Joe tried to lead Abe into conversation as well, but the older man said little beyond "no" and "yes."

After supper, Joe escorted Angelina back to the convalescent home.

On the way, he told her about his family. "Everyone still lives at home, except for Mike, who is overseas."

"What is your house like?"

"It's a grand, impressive home made of brick."

"Brick?"

"Yes. Most of the houses in Ontario are made of brick."

"Why would that be?"

"It's more humid there than it is here and brick doesn't rot."

Joe went on. "There is always food on our table; my mother is an excellent cook. We never went hungry during the Depression, like so many other Canadians did. There was always fruit to eat; all we had to do was pick it. Down east we grow apples and peaches and grapes and pears."

Her mind travelled back in time to when she had first tasted a pear. It had been the Christmas she was nine years old. She and her family had taken the cutter and gone to her Taunte Ginter's house in the city. When they got there, Taunte had handed each of her nieces and nephews a banana, an orange and a pear. At first none of the children had known what to do with them. They had never before seen such things. Encouraged by her aunt to taste the fruit, Angelina bit into the pear. It had been wonderful, a bit like an apple, yet sweeter and more granular, like white sugar. Angelina had thought her Taunte must be quite rich indeed.

"It must be wonderful to live in a land where such fruit grows for the picking," Angelina remarked dreamily.

"Oh, it is. Still, the orchards in Ontario are nothing compared to what we had back in the Old Country. In Poland, we had the most exquisite gardens." Joe reflected for a moment. "We had servants as well. My mother is descended from Prussian nobility."

"Why did your folks move away? Move to Canada?"

"A dictator took over our country. So my family, along with many others, emigrated. I was only five years old, but I remember the ship and feeling seasick. I remember my mother putting cool cloths on my head and crooning, '*Mnie Jitsi*' to me. In Polish that means "my child."

"It sounds like your mother loves you very much."

"Yes. My mother is a very loving person. My whole family is. If you married me, you would be loved and embraced by all of them."

Angelina smiled at the vision. *How wonderful that would be.*

Just short of the city, the couple climbed a knoll that gave them a view of the lights below. Joe stopped and took her in his arms.

"Let's dance," he said, and began to sing softly:

"Don't know why there's no sun up in the sky,
stormy weather,
since my gal and I ain't together
it's raining all the time..."

He led; she followed.

At the end of the song, Joe murmured in Angelina's ear. "Yes, darling, it would be raining all the time without you.

Please marry me," he pled. "I will make you the happiest woman alive."

This time she accepted.

They walked hand in hand into town, down Avenue A and to the door of the convalescent home. Angelina felt alive and very happy. She had found her dream man. Now all they had to do was announce their engagement to her parents.

"*Nijch. na!*" Papa exploded upon hearing the news. "No marriage!"

"Na. He is the *Enjelsch,*" Mama protested.

The fact that Joe was Polish meant nothing. In their minds he was "the English." Margaretha and Abe had taken it for granted that Angelina, like the rest of the family, would one day choose a man from among the *Plautdietsch*. Now here she was, wanting to marry a man who was not only English but also a "soldier man," and a Catholic as well. *Na. Na!*

Papa didn't care about being *nijch oppnament.* He ordered Joe to leave his house.

3

WEEKS HAD PASSED and Margaretha was worried. She knew that Angelina continued to see the young English man. Angelina's sister Betty had informed her of that. Betty had also told her that one time when she had gone to visit Angelina, she had caught the couple kissing. Margaretha didn't know what to do. She didn't like Angelina being with Joe but she was concerned that if she didn't allow her to marry, Angelina might decide to "live in sin" like Margaretha's sister Sosche had done years earlier.

Sosche—Sarah—had, at fourteen, asked her Mama and Papa for permission to marry the boy she loved. Sosche's request was denied. She and the boy—sixteen—were too young, they said. So Sosche proceeded to get herself pregnant. Still she was refused. Sosche had the baby and moved in with the boy in defiance.

Her sister had been the talk of the village. Whenever Margaretha went for a walk with Sosche, she had seen fingers being pointed and lips moving behind hands—"For shame!"

Sosche was Margaretha's favourite sister so it had bothered her deeply. She had felt ashamed for her sister.

Then Sosche had conceived again. Following the birth of this second baby, Mama and Papa had finally relented.

Margaretha did not want a repeat of this with her own daughter. She told Angelina to bring Joe to visit her during a time when Papa would be working.

"If you were to marry Angelina," she asked Joe, "would you make her become the Catholic?"

"Oh, no. Never!" Joe placated Margaretha. "I will never make her become what she is not willing to be."

Well, he does *seem to be a nice young man, even if he is the English. And he's always so well-dressed. And I've seen that he is a good worker.* "All right, then. I will give my word on the paper."

But Abe wiped his hands of the whole affair. "I will not sign the paper. It is not just that he is the English and a soldier man," he insisted. "There is something else; there is something about that man that isn't all right," he said. "If Angelina marries him, it will not be because of me."

Because Angelina was underaged, she needed two signatures to marry. She got the second from Grandmother Ginter.

Joe talked her into quitting her job at the convalescent home. "You won't need to work anymore," he said. "Once we're married, the air force will give you a maintenance allowance."

4

THE WEDDING WAS three weeks away. Angelina made invitations by hand then rode out on her sorrel mare, Polly, to deliver them to neighbouring friends and relatives. Having stopped to chat along the way, she lost track of time and it was dark when she got home.

While she was gone, Joe had come out to the farm. Upon hearing her horse's arrival, he ran out to meet her.

"Where were you?" he demanded, roughly pulling her off her horse.

"I've been delivering invitations," she answered.

"It took you this long? You're lying!" His eyes flashed like silver lightning across a black prairie sky.

Angelina shivered and began backing away.

"I know what you've been doing. You've been out gallivanting with another man, haven't you?" he accused, advancing towards her.

"No, no. That's not true!" Angelina gasped. "No!"

"Yes, it is," Joe snarled, shaking her.

"Let me go!"

Freeing herself from his grasp, Angelina fled to the house and up the stairs to her room. Slamming the door, she leaned against it. She was frightened. She had just seen a side of Joe she had never suspected.

Her papa had a mean streak in him, too, and she had suffered ill treatment from him many times because of it. Angelina remembered a night he had locked her in the tool shed for not eating the turnips on her plate. It had been the longest night of her life. She had been so cold and so frightened. In the morning she ate the turnips waiting for her on the table. Yet another time, Papa had started beating her with a horse harness because the younger children had made a mess of the house. "But Papa," she had pleaded on her hands and knees, "I wasn't even home. I was with you and Mama in the city!"

Still, even as bad-tempered as Papa sometimes was, she didn't see in him the evil she had just spotted in Joe's eyes.

Angelina waited until she was sure Joe had left before coming down the stairs and announcing to her mother, "I'm not marrying him."

"What do you mean!" Margaretha asked.

"He accused me of cheating on him and he was going to hit me! I'm so glad I found out what he was really like before it was too late."

The next day Joe returned to the farm bearing a bouquet of flowers. He begged Margaretha for a chance to speak to Angelina.

"I...I'm sorry. I guess I just lost my head," he said when he saw her. "It's just that you're so beautiful I don't think straight sometimes. But it will never happen again. I swear. Please give me another chance, my angel."

"No. I don't love you after all. I thought I did but now I know I don't." Angelina walked away.

"Angelina, please!" Joe called after her.

Angelina walked into the house.

Joe parked himself on the outside step.

"I think you should give the young man another chance," Margaretha contended. "Papa doesn't hit me, Joe won't hit you. He's probably just feeling a little nervous about getting married, that's all. Men are like that."

"But I don't want to marry him anymore. I thought I loved him but now I know I don't."

"It's too late. You promised him you would, so you must. I know, too, you have sinned with him. Betty told me. Now it is your duty to marry him."

Yes, she had sinned with Joe, though she didn't recall Betty having caught her. Joe had begged her to have sex with him almost from the time they had met, but she had resisted. Then, after she had agreed to marry him, he had said, "It's all right now. We're engaged."

Still Angelina had hesitated.

"If you loved me, *really* loved me," Joe insisted, "you wouldn't make me wait. Darling, a man has his needs."

A man has his needs. A half-buried memory from long ago had flashed through her head—a memory of unbearable pain. Angelina had trembled with the recollection of it but knew she could stall Joe no longer. She was now engaged to him and...a man had his needs. She had felt she had no choice but to give in.

Just as she now knew she had no choice but to accept his apology and resume the wedding plans.

She was sixteen and Joe, twenty-one.

5

ANGELINA STRUGGLED UP the walk leading to what was to be her new home. Joe, running ahead, had left her behind to cope with the suitcases. He was anxious to be reunited with his family, whom he hadn't seen in over a year.

Joe and Angelina had been married only a few months when Joe had been reassigned, this time to Camp Borden, sixty miles north of Toronto, Ontario. A month later he had mailed Angelina a one-way train ticket to New Toronto. He asked for and received a few days leave to meet Angelina at the train station and bring her to her new home with his folks.

A neighbour woman in her early twenties approached the young newlywed where she had stopped to rest for a momen with the suitcases. "Ah yow Jow's new woif?" she asked in a heavy British accent.

"Yes, I am."

"Luke, thees is none of moi business, but yow jest a

little slip of a thing, so oi figger oi should warn yow. If yow know whot's good for yow, yow'll turn around and go bock from wha yow came from. Thot family do nowt but foight and ahgue awl dye long."

The neighbour glanced at the open door then quickly retreated back into her own yard.

What have I got myself into? Angelina wondered as she walked through the door.

Everyone was crowded around Joe, slapping him on the back, hugging him. A middle-aged woman caressed his cheeks, tears of joy running down her own. No one paid Angelina any heed as she walked into the house. Several minutes passed before Joe slipped her hand into his and announced, "This is my wife, everyone—Angelina."

He gave her a deep kiss. They all cheered. Glasses were raised. *"Nazdrowie!"*

Then Joe went back to visiting and Angelina was left on her own to discern who was who. Joe had previously told her that he had four siblings, a sister—fourteen-year old Bernice—and three brothers. The oldest, at twenty-three, was fighting overseas.

Not counting Joe and herself, there were seven people there, two women and a baby, two men, an adolescent boy and a teenaged girl. Angelina gathered that the large, heavy-boned woman who had fussed so over Joe's arrival must be his mother, Mrs. Jaslo, and the older man sitting in the armchair and pouring himself another vodka, her husband, Joe's father. The younger man and boy were likely Joe's brothers and the girl, his sister. Angelina wasn't sure who the young woman holding the baby was. She didn't look anything like the others. She was tall and slim with short, fiery red hair set in a wave. Angelina decided to make her acquaintance.

"What a beautiful baby you have," Angelina said to the woman. "Is it a boy?"

"Yeah."

"Are you by chance married to one of Joe's brothers?"

"Yeah, I'm Francis. I'm married to Mike."

"Mike is the man who's talking to Joe?"

"No. Mike is overseas."

"You must miss him."

"What I miss is living with people who speak English and eat normal food. As soon as this bloody war is over, Mike and I are going to get a place of our own. I'll see to that. If the army gave me a bigger maintenance allowance I wouldn't wait, I'd move out now."

Francis walked away abruptly, ending the conversation.

The rest of the family kept glancing Angelina's way and speaking among themselves in a language she didn't understand. Joe had said he was Polish, so Angelina assumed that must be what they were speaking.

Finally, the adolescent boy came up to where she was sitting and introduced himself in English. "Hello, I'm Edward," he said.

"I'm pleased to meet you, Edward." Angelina responded with real sincerity, happy to at last encounter someone who acknowledged her. "You must be one of Joe's brothers?"

"Yes, his youngest. I'm sixteen."

Edward wore glasses and had a scholarly look about him. Like the rest of his family, he had seal-brown curly hair.

"You are from Saskatchewan, the prairies?" Edward inquired.

"I am. Have you heard of Saskatoon?"

"Yes."

"Well, my family lives near there; just a few miles out, actually."

"Have you ever been to Ontario before?"

"No, never. This is the first time I've ever been out of Saskatchewan."

"Well, I hope you don't miss home too much."

I hope so too, Angelina thought.

At that moment, Joe grabbed Angelina's hand and said, "Supper is ready."

He led her to the large table in the dining room.

The family began taking their seats, with Mr. Jaslo at the head of the table. Angelina sat between Joe on her right and Edward on her left.

Joe's mother sat just long enough to partake in the prayer, quickly blessed herself, and then, as others began buttering their bread, headed back to the kitchen. A moment later she returned with what looked like beet soup, placed it on the table and then quickly ran back and retrieved a pot of chicken soup. A third dish held noodles. Mrs. Jaslo then went around the table ladling out soup to everyone. Some received the beet, others the chicken.

Why is she giving different kinds of soup to everybody? Angelina wondered.

Mrs. Jaslo reached her.

"Barszcz? Hen?" the woman asked.

Angelina looked at her in confusion.

Joe, deep in conversation with the man beside him—Angelina assumed it must be another of his brothers, didn't notice.

Mrs. Jaslo threw Angelina an impatient look.

"Barszcz?" she repeated, *"Hen?"* She set down the pots of soup and then, bending each arm as into wings, she began flapping them. *"Hen?"*

"I...uh," Angelina stuttered nervously.

Edward intercepted. "My mother is asking you if you'd like beet soup or chicken soup."

"Oh, oh! Chicken, please," she answered, flapping her own wings emphatically.

"Rosol z kury i kluski," Edward told his mother.

Mrs. Jaslo filled Angelina's bowl with the hot soup.

Angelina watched agog as the woman continued ladling out the two varieties of soup. It reminded her of a restaurant. At home you didn't get a choice like that. You ate what was put in front of you.

Joe ceased talking for a moment to fork more food into his mouth.

Angelina decided to ask him the name of the brother sitting beside him.

"It's Steve, Steve Jr.," Joe answered with a scowl.

At that moment, a piece of bread aimed at Joe came flying across the table, thrown by the girl Angelina had assumed must be Bernice.

Joe let loose a string of expletives. Bernice stuck her tongue out at him. Joe rose from the table and headed for his sister, vengeance in his eye. Evading him, she jumped out of her chair and began running around the table. As he gained on her, she ducked behind their mother. Joe reached around her, trying to get to the girl.

My goodness, what kind of family have I got myself into? Angelina worried. *They act like a bunch of hooligans.*

In the family she had grown up in, meals had been a solemn affair, something to be thankful for. You didn't scream or run about in the house, never mind around the table!

Steve Sr. spoke. *"Cichy!"*

The din settled.

Once the first course was finished the bowls were removed and then one dish after another was placed on the table. There was sauerkraut and sausage sautéed together and seasoned with sweet, red paprika; a bowl of what Angelina knew as *warenekje*, but what they were calling *pierogi*; dainty cabbage rolls; a platter of succulent roast pork; creamy mashed potatoes and gravy; and boiled cabbage sprinkled with caraway seed.

"Nazdrowie!" Joe said.

Angelina raised her glass of wine with the others. Joe had told her of a loving, welcoming family. Perhaps this large elaborate meal was their way of greeting her.

After supper, Angelina stood up to help with the clearing of the table, but Joe grabbed her arm and said in a low growl, "I want to talk to you. Alone."

He manoeuvred her into the bathroom. "Now, I want to know why were you so anxious to know Steve's name?"

"What? Why, because I was able to figure almost everyone else out. I talked to Francis, and Edward introduced himself, but I didn't know Steve's name. I figured he must be your brother because you said you had three, and there's a similarity between you two, but no one told me his name."

"I see. Well, I want to make something very clear right now," Joe replied coldly, "if you ever try to flirt with him, he'll tell me."

"*Flirt* with him? Why would I want to flirt with him? He's your brother!"

"Oh? You mean to say that if he wasn't, you would?"

"What? No. No! That's not what I'm trying to say. I'm not interested in Steve."

"Well, I'm just warning you that he'll let me know if you are. Now, let's go sit down and visit with the others."

"But what about the dishes? I should help your mother."

"No. I haven't seen you for over a month. I want you with me.

Angelina sat with Joe but may as well have sat alone. He chattered away in Polish with his family as though Angelina wasn't even there. Her eyes swept the room. Joe had described the house as big and fancy. But judging by what she had seen so far, it seemed rather small and plain. She would have liked to wander around and have a better look at it.

I wonder how many bedrooms there are? Francis, Bernice and the baby probably share one of the rooms. Steve and Edward likely share another. I wonder what our bedroom looks like? There aren't any house plants in the living room or the dining room. I hope Joe's mother won't mind if I put a couple in our room. If I just knew where our room was, I could at least put the suitcases in it.

"Joe," Angelina finally got a word in edgewise, "where's our room?"

"Our room? What do you mean *our* room?"

"Where we sleep," she answered.

"We'll sleep on the hide-a-bed in the living room."

"But I thought..."

Joe was no longer listening. He was back conversing with his father.

ANGELINA SOON DISCOVERED that the feast she had partaken of on the first evening was not just served on special occasions. Josephine, as Angelina came to know Mrs. Jaslo, always cooked like this, catering daily to each family member's tastes. Angelina felt sorry for her new mother-in-law. She spent most of her time in the kitchen with no help from Bernice or Francis. *No one at home would ever expect Mama to work so hard in the kitchen.*

But as much as Josephine did for her family, she seemed to receive no appreciation. It was as though everyone expected it of her. Not only that, they all hollered at her too. On Angelina's third day there the family had been seated around the table when Steve Sr. abruptly asked Josephine a question. The woman had answered in a belligerent tone, whereupon he had stood from his chair with his fist raised at her. Fortunately, she had managed to evade him and he had eventually cooled down.

Angelina had been shocked. *Papa would never raise his hand to Mama in anger.*

Joe had spoken of a loving family, of their affectionate ways, but other than Josephine's spoiling of her children Angelina had yet to see it.

"My folks will love you and welcome you with open arms," Joe had told Angelina back in Saskatchewan.

That didn't seem to be true either. Other than Edward, the family continued to ignore her. Though all but Joe's parents could speak good English, the family conversed mostly in Polish. When Angelina tried to engage one of them in conversation, they either replied with one-word sentences or simply walked away. She commented on it to Joe one night when they were alone.

"I don't think they like me," she added.

"It's just your imagination, and the reason we speak Polish is because that's the language we feel most comfortable with. If it bothers you that much, you're just going to have to learn how to speak it too. But I think your main problem is that you've just got too much time on your hands. Which reminds me. I've been meaning to discuss something with you. I've asked my mother to teach you how to cook."

"Teach me how to cook? I already know how to cook."

Angelina protested. "I've been cooking since I was a young girl."

"Yes, I realize that, my dear, but most of the meals you learned how to prepare at home were fried and bland. Of course, I'm not blaming your mother for that. Your family was poor and couldn't afford good food."

"Well, I...it wasn't just from my mother that I learned how to cook. My first job at the age of fourteen was cooking in a restaurant. And the customers were very happy with my—"

"You call the slop served in Canada food?" Joe interposed. "When I speak of good cuisine, I am referring to meals like my mother makes, the type of cooking done in the Old Country." He pinched his right hand together, fingers to thumb, and kissed them. "*Mmm.* Superb. In Poland the women aren't lazy. They know how to prepare good food; they don't just hurriedly throw it together like the women here do."

"I'm not lazy! I've worked hard all my life."

"Oh, my dear! Did you think I was implying that *you* are lazy? Of course you're not lazy, my little angel." Joe stroked her arm. "It's merely that you haven't been taught any better, and you are young as well as somewhat simple. My mother will be happy to take you under her wing and teach you."

Angelina sighed. She had come to realize that she couldn't win debates with Joe. He was smart and knew how to win.

Angelina felt a flash of anger towards her mother. *It's Mama's fault I'm here. She made me marry him.* But it was too late; she *was* married, and had no choice but to do as her husband asked. It was her wifely duty.

She would try, she would try very hard to satisfy Joe and learn how to make the kind of meals that he liked.

The days passed and Joe's furlough came to an end. When he walked out the door, Angelina cried. He had been her only lifeline with these people who didn't like her.

6

THE MORNING JOE left, Angelina went into the kitchen and stood by her mother-in-law's side to learn her recipes. Josephine glanced at her and narrowed her eyes. She muttered words that, though foreign, clearly indicated that she resented Angelina's presence.

Angelina gulped.

"Obserwuja mnie," Josephine said gruffly.

"I—I don't understand." Angelina turned her hands palm up and shook her head.

The larger woman's heavy eyebrows knitted together in disapproval. *"Obserwuja!"* she repeated, more loudly this time.

"Wait, wait," Angelina said, holding up a hand. She quickly ran into the dining room where Bernice was eating a piece of toast. "Quickly, quickly, what does *obserwuja* mean?" she anxiously asked thc girl.

Bernice looked at her as though she were a simpleton. "It means, 'watch.'"

"Oh! Thank you. *Thank you,*" Angelina gasped in relief.

She rushed back to Josephine's side to begin carefully observing her mother-in-law's movements. She was able to discern that Josephine was making chicken stock, likely for what they called *Rosol z kury i kluski*—one of Joe's favourites. Josephine set a whole chicken on to boil. It had to be an old hen, Angelina would later learn, as young birds didn't have enough flavour.

Angelina's mother-in-law threw some pickling spice into the pot and then began quartering carrots and stalks of celery.

Angelina, thinking she was doing Josephine a favour, began peeling the onion she saw sitting among the vegetables waiting for the pot.

"No. No," Josephine protested, grabbing the onion out of Angelina's hand. She cut it in half and threw it, peel and all, into the pot. It wasn't until months later that Angelina was able to understand why Josephine had done that. The peel contributed to the broth's flavour.

After simmering all day, the chicken in its broth was placed in the fridge to cool. In the morning, Josephine skimmed off the fat that had gelled over night. She then strained it and put it, along with the chicken—boned and skinned—into a clean pot. She added fresh carrots, celery and onion—peeled and quartered this time—into the broth to make soup. Josephine then made the egg noodle dough, rolled it out, and sliced it into thin strips so that it could be boiled just before supper and added to each bowl at the table.

Angelina took to keeping a scribbler at her side at all times to write down Polish words she heard the others speak. When Edward came home from school, she would ask him the meanings of the words. Angelina avoided asking Bernice questions. The last time she had, Bernice had snapped, "Do you always have to ask me what things mean all the time? Can't you figure it out for yourself?"

Angelina found herself alone with Steve one afternoon. He was in the army but, like Joe, received occasional leaves. She tried to strike up a conversation with him.

"I understand you were four when your family immigrated to Canada. Do you remember anything about Poland?"

"Yes," Steve answered, avoiding her gaze.

"What do you remember?"

"I remember my grandmother."

"She stayed behind in Poland?"

"Yes."

"You must miss her sometimes."

Steve turned his head to look Angelina straight in the eye. "Why are you asking me all these questions? Are you trying to flirt with me or something?"

Angelina turned red with embarrassment. "Flirt? I...I wasn't trying to flirt. I was just trying to talk with you."

"Well, Joe warned me about you. You better not be flirting. Besides, I don't talk to Nazis."

"Nazis? What—?"

Steve got up and marched out of the room.

Later that day, Bernice went up to Angelina and said, "You know my brother and two of my cousins are overseas right now fighting filthy Nazi Germans. I bet none of the men in *your* family are."

"No, they're busy farming." Angelina had kept quiet about the fact that going to war went against the Mennonite faith. No sense rubbing it in that she wasn't Catholic as they were.

"Well, I think that maybe they stay behind because they don't want to fight the Krauts since they are Germans too!"

"We're not German; we're Pennsylvania Dutch."

Francis, overhearing the conversation, decided to add her two cents. "Is that so? According to Joe, your family speaks German."

"The language is called *Plautdietsch,* Low German," Angelina said, "but we're actually Dutch, not German."

"Right, and I'm a Pole who speaks Russian," Bernice said snidely. "Don't lie! Your white hair and ghost-face give you away. You look just like those Nazis. I've seen pictures of them."

Josephine, also in the room, couldn't understand the entire conversation but was able to pick up enough words to get the general gist of it.

"Nazi," she hissed without any problem.

Angelina burst into tears.

"It's not *true!* I'm not a Nazi! I'll...I'll send for my birth certificate. I'll prove it to you!"

She fled the room.

Later that day, Edward, having overheard the conversation, took Angelina aside and apologized for his family's cruel words.

"My mother came from gentry. Back in Poland when she was a young girl, her family had riches, beautiful gardens and servants—but between the Germans and Russians, they eventually lost most of it. The two bordering countries kept stealing more and more of Poland's land. In 1926, a dictator came into power and things got worse. Mom and Dad, Mike and Steve, and Joe—Bernice and I weren't born yet—moved to Canada, but my mother's parents, my grandparents, chose to remain in Poland. Then, five years ago, in 1939, my mother received a letter from a friend still living in the Old Country. The Germans had seized my grandparents' house. They took my grandmother outside and smashed her head repeatedly against her once lovely garden wall. My grandfather was forced to watch. He died a few days later from a heart attack."

"Oh, no!" Angelina cried, tears of sympathy filling her eyes. She hugged Edward. "Oh, Edward, I'm sorry. I'm so sorry. I didn't know. But, please believe me. I'm not German."

Angelina vowed that she would try extra hard to be more kind and tolerant towards the family. She would also prove to them that she wasn't a Nazi. That night she sat down with pen and paper and wrote a letter to the Department of Vital Statistics.

May 9, 1944

Dear Sir,

Please can you help me? I got married eight months ago. My husband is in the air force, so I am living with his folks here in New Toronto. But they hate me. They hate me so much because they think I am German. They say I am a Nazi. But I am not German and I am not a Nazi. I'm Pennsylvania Dutch. I told them that, but they don't believe me. Please sir, please can you send me a certificate that shows I'm really Dutch so that I can show it to them and they'll like me?

I was born on Jan. 10, 1927 in Warman, Saskatchewan. My father's name is Abe Bickert. He was born in Aberdeen, Saskatchewan. My mother's maiden name was Margaretha Ginter. She was born in Osler, Saskatchewan.

Thank you, sir. Thank you so very, very much.

Sincerely,
Angelina Jaslo

7

ANGELINA DID HER best, but it seemed the nicer she was toward her in-laws, the worse they treated her. She became little more than a servant, an unpaid one at that. Angelina spent most of her day helping Josephine with the cooking and cleaning, though she was never permitted to do any of the former alone.

"I don't trust you. You don't do a good enough job," Josephine would say. When company came, Josephine would forbid Angelina to sit at the dining room table with them. "We won't have our guests eat with a Nazi."

Somehow Josephine picked up the word "stupid" and began using it to address Angelina. Now, whenever Josephine wanted her, she would call out, "Hey, stupid!"

Before long Bernice picked up the habit as well.

It was humiliating for Angelina. She tearfully complained to Joe about it one day when he was home on leave.

"I'm sure they're just joking with you and...well, you can't entirely blame them if they *do* view you as dim at times. Even I have to admit that sometimes you do some rather strange things."

Angelina's mind drifted back to when she was ten...

She and her family were getting ready to go out visiting.

"Hurry up, Angelina," her father yelled at her.

His impatience made Angelina nervous. Now where did I put my gloves? *She ran from room to room, looking.* Oh God, please, please tell me, where are my gloves? *She knew she'd be in trouble if she didn't find them. She heard the sound of her father's heavy boots as he ascended the stairs.* Oh no! Oh no!

"What is taking you so long?" he hollered.

"I'm coming, Papa. I'm coming," she quivered.

He was in the room. "What are you looking for?" he growled.

"I can't find my gloves," she whimpered.

He looked at her as though she had lost her head. "Oh du best daumelskopp me'jal! *There they are right on your hands!"*

Yes, it did appear at times as though she were a numbskull. But it wasn't just nervousness that contributed to her problem, Angelina reflected. Sometimes it was because she had trouble hearing too. One time her papa had come up the stairs, roaring mad, and had cuffed her because she hadn't answered when he had called her.

"I didn't hear you, Papa. I didn't hear you!" she had cried.

"That's probably because you're off in your dream world again!" he had retorted...

Joe continued. "But it's certainly not your fault you're simple. And I agree it isn't right of my family to rub your nose in it. You did, after all, receive only a Grade 6 education. I'll have a talk with my mother."

His words only made her feel worse. *Why was I ever so foolish as to tell him I only went to Grade 6?*

She had frequently missed classes during her school years. It had been one thing after another. There had been health issues. In Grade 1 she had contracted whooping cough; a couple of years later, the travelling doctor diagnosed rickets. At the beginning of Grade 6 she had begun to have frequent nosebleeds. "Stop that!" her teacher had demanded, vexed. "I'm tired of your nosebleeds. You must be doing something to cause them. Either quit bleeding or stay home." Since Angelina hadn't known how to prevent her nose from bleeding, she had often stayed away. "It's just as well," Mama and Papa had said. "You're needed at home."

If only! she now thought to herself. *If only I could write better! If only I could explain myself better! If only I could hear better. But God made me like this. I know the Lord must have a reason. But why? It makes me look so stupid!*

Angelina, however, was not the only one the family disliked; they didn't much care for Francis either.

Joe and Josephine called Francis "one of those English girls." Actually, she was Irish, but "English, Irish, Scottish, all the same—lazy women," they said. They didn't dare say any of this to Francis' face, though. She had a fiery temper and refused to put up with any taunting.

Steve Sr. once told Angelina, "I wish you were the Irish, and the other girl, Francis, the German. Then I like you. But I don't like Nazi."

8

A COUPLE OF MONTHS after Angelina moved in with the family, Steve Sr.'s cousin Alice came to visit. Alice was held in high esteem. Well-to-do and highly educated, she had been to many places in the world before finally settling down as a doctor's wife. Alice was a no-nonsense type of woman who said things the way she saw them.

When Alice saw Angelina serving the meal while the rest of the family sat, and she heard their insistence that Angelina was a Nazi, she spoke up.

"You bunch of idiots. How can you be so ignorant? She's no more of a Nazi than I am. I've been to Germany and that is *not* German she is speaking. If she says she's Dutch, then that's probably what she is. I'm ashamed of the way you pick on that poor girl."

Alice then said to Angelina, "You sit and *I* shall serve."

No one objected, not even Bernice.

Angelina felt a ray of hope. *Now, finally, they will be*

nicer to me. But much to Angelina's dismay, once Alice left, things returned to the way they had been before.

ANGELINA WAS EXCITED the day she saw the envelope addressed to her from the Department of Statistics. She opened it anxiously. There was an orange document inside. Her birth certificate. With shaking hands she read the words. She reached the part that said "racial origin." She read the words: "Dutch descent."

"Look everyone, look!" Angelina announced excitedly, holding it up for everyone to see. "See! Here's my proof that I'm not German!"

"Dutch, German, there's little difference," Joe, who was home, said.

"But there *is!*" Angelina cried in frustration.

"What do *you* know? You're too stupid to know anything." Bernice said. She covered her mouth. "Oh, sorry. I'm not supposed to use that word. It might hurt your feelings."

Suddenly a loud, firm voice rose above the others. "Leave her alone," Steve Sr. had come to her defense. "Remember what Alice say? Dutch is not the German Nazi."

Quiet ensued—the patriarch had spoken. Henceforth the family took more care not to criticize Angelina in his presence.

Edward, who had heard Joe's and Bernice's words, waited until he had an opportunity to be alone with Angelina before saying, "You know, they say you're stupid, but you're not. You're actually very smart. Look how quickly you are learning Polish words, understanding them, speaking them. A person who isn't very smart wouldn't be able to do that."

"Oh, do you really think so?" Angelina said, grasping for reassurance. "But maybe you're just saying that to make me feel better?"

"No. I really mean it. And you know something else? I think my sister is jealous of you."

"Jealous of me? Whatever for?"

"Because you're nice and you're pretty and she isn't. You know, sometimes I get so fed up with my family. Someone is always fighting with someone else. Other people don't do that. I've been to other people's homes. I'm just looking forward to finishing school so I can leave home."

"What are you hoping to be?"

"A teacher."

"I think you'll make a fine teacher," Angelina told him. "You have a kind heart."

"My brother is so lucky. I wish I had a girlfriend like you."

"You're so sweet, Edward," Angelina said, giving her young brother-in-law a peck on the cheek.

9

ANGELINA WOKE EARLY one morning, before dawn, to cramps. *My monthly is here,* she thought. She wadded some rags together and pinned them onto her panties. Within minutes they were soaked. Angelina was surprised. Her period wasn't usually this heavy. In fact, the past few times they had been extra light. The cramps became painful, then excruciating. As Angelina staggered towards the bath-room, the flow turned to a gush.

She was instantly transported back to when she was six years old—*"Mama, help me. Help me! Uncle Peita hurt me." She reached out for her mother.*

The ground tipped and Angelina crumpled.

"Angelina, Angelina," she heard the voice through a distance. Her eyes searched through the fog. "Mama?"

"No, it's Francis. Lie still. The doctor's coming."

Presently there was a knock on the door. Francis went to answer it.

"Hello, doctor. Yes, she's right over here."

Angelina lay on the floor covered with a blanket. A pillow supported her head. Josephine and Bernice peered around the corner.

The doctor checked Angelina's vital signs. "I think she should go to the hospital. Is there anyone here who can take her?"

When Francis said there wasn't, the doctor took her himself.

At the hospital, Angelina learned she had had a miscarriage and had been about four months pregnant.

"But—but I didn't even know I was carrying! I still had my monthlies. How could that be?"

"Sometimes that happens," the doctor told her.

Then she was left alone in the room to think.

I was a mommy and I didn't even know it. In five months I could have had a baby of my own to hold and to love, and to love me back.

Tears flowed down her cheeks and onto her pillow.

She was in the hospital for four days, during which time no one came to see her. She was lonely but also relieved—at least no one here harped at her. Then Joe came home and asked that Angelina be released into his and his mother's care. The doctor wanted to keep her in longer—there had been hemorrhaging, and she had had to have blood transfusions—but agreed to let her go under the condition that she rest.

The next morning, Josephine said, "I think it just you feel sorry for yourself. In Poland, woman has baby and next day she work in field."

Joe agreed with his mother. "Get up. You've lain there long enough."

That night she was back in the hospital. This time the doctor kept her in until she had recuperated.

10

IT HAD BEEN six months, six long months of hell. She had tried so hard to be nice, to fit in, to be accepted. But it had all been to no avail. The final straw came during one of Joe's leaves. Josephine had been arguing with him. They had been talking too rapidly for Angelina to get all the words, but it had something to do with church.

Following the dispute, Joe had growled at Angelina, "I want you to start going to Mass. You will go this Sunday!"

"No. I will not. You promised my parents that I would not have to go to your church."

Joe pulled back his arm and slapped Angelina hard across the face. "How dare you talk back to me! I said you're going!"

Angelina put a hand on to her stinging cheek. "No, Joe. I will not. You can kill me, but I will not go to your church!"

Joe turned on his heel and walked out.

When Joe had struck her, Angelina had caught a quick glance of the smirking, satisfied look on her mother-in-law's face. That had hurt more than the slap and Angelina had finally admitted defeat.

She waited until Joe had returned to base, then, using her maintenance allowance, she rented a furnished room on the other side of New Toronto.

The room, located on the upstairs floor of a house, was plain and somewhat dreary-looking, but Angelina was undaunted. She was skilled at transforming the drab into the attractive. She had spent much time helping her mother fix up one house after another as they followed Abe in his endless quest for work during the Depression.

Angelina manoeuvred the hide-a-bed from against the wall into the centre of the room, effectively transforming one room into three: a kitchen with a table and a hot plate on one end, a living room with an end table and cabinet radio on the other, and at night, a bedroom in the middle. She took down the sombre, cream-coloured curtains and hand-sewed bright new ones—lemon-yellow with aqua lace—to take their place.

I'm free. I'm free!

Angelina soon made friends with the landlady, June, who was somewhere in her twenties and had a young boy. She learned that June's husband was fighting overseas and that she rented out the upstairs room to help make ends meet. Angelina offered to look after little Timmy for June whenever she needed to step out.

On Joe's next leave he came to see Angelina, demanding to know why she had moved out of his parents' house. She told him she couldn't take living with his family anymore.

"I want you to stay there," he insisted, "so Mom can keep an eye on you and make sure you don't go out with other men while I'm gone."

"I told you, I'm not interested in other men."

"Well, they're interested in *you*. I've seen how they look at you. You're so beautiful they can't help but look. But I've also seen how you look into their eyes when they talk to you. You even did that with me when we first met."

"But—but I do that with *everybody*. That's just the way I talk to people!"

"A decent woman doesn't do that. A decent woman averts her eyes when she speaks to men. If you had been raised Roman Catholic, you would have been taught that. But since you weren't, how am I to trust you alone?"

"You can trust me!" Angelina declared, feeling increasingly frustrated.

"You say that, but how can I? You weren't a virgin when we met. That right there indicates you have loose morals."

"That wasn't my fault!" Angelina protested. "I told you. I was raped!"

"Well, that would never have happened to a good Catholic girl. You likely enticed him, batting your eyes, wiggling your butt."

"That's not true! I didn't!"

"You probably didn't even realize you were doing it. You can't blame the man; men have their needs. It states in the Bible that woman was placed on Earth to serve man and his needs." He paused. "But we are side-tracking. I want you to pack up. I'm taking you back to my folks."

Angelina was firm. "No. I refuse to go back there! Your family doesn't like me. And they say that we're not really married anyway because I'm not a Catholic!"

Joe narrowed his eyes at her. His family's refusal to accept the legitimacy of his marriage irritated him, regardless of what the Church thought on the matter.

"Well, if you would quit being so stubborn and become a Roman Catholic..." He paced up and down the aisle between the couch and the cabinet radio for a few minutes in thought.

"All right, I will allow you to stay here but I insist that my mother escort you when you go shopping. And if I ever find out that you go without her..."

To this Angelina agreed.

11

ANGELINA APPLIED HER makeup carefully. Joe had received a weekend pass and they were going dancing tonight. And not to just any dance hall but to the Casa Loma ballroom.

They had taken the trolley to downtown Toronto that morning and shopped for the perfect dress for her to wear for the occasion. Angelina had tried on several, but the full, rose-petal pink chiffon that lent colour to her fine ivory skin was the one Joe had decided on. Its crinoline emphasized Angelina's tiny waist, and when she twirled the gown floated up to her knees and around in a silky cloud. To compliment the dress they had bought pumps in a matching colour.

He really could be very sweet sometimes.

But she knew the main reason he had bought her the clothes was to show her off. He often told her how beautiful she was and how proud he was to be the envy of other men. These words of praise made her feel good—just as her papa's words used to make her feel. (I've since asked my mother why she stayed. She said it was because she felt it was her duty.)

Angelina heard the sound of Joe's footsteps coming up the stairs. He had been visiting over at his mother's house.

Joe quietly closed the door behind him and started walking towards her. His face was tight, his eyes dark with anger.

Angelina involuntarily backed away. "What's wrong?" she asked.

Joe grabbed her by the shoulders and began shaking her. "You know damn well what's wrong," he growled.

"Honest, I don't. What did I do wrong this time?"

"You've been flirting with men."

"No, no!"

"Don't lie to me, woman!" Joe said, backhanding her across the face. "My mother saw you! She said that you were batting your eyes and flipping your hair at a sales clerk last week."

"What are you talking about? No. I didn't!" Angelina insisted.

"You're saying my mother lied?" He struck her again.

Her nose began to bleed.

"You probably gave him your address too, didn't you?" He shoved her against the wall. *"Didn't you!"*

"No! Honest to God, Joe, I didn't!" Angelina cried.

Joe banged the back of her head against the wall.

"I swear, I didn't do anything wrong. I swear! Please, please don't hit me anymore!"

How many times had she cried those words to her father in subjugation when *he* had hit her?

"You didn't cheat on me?" Joe asked.

"No!"

"You love me?"

"Yes."

"You swear?"

"Yes."

"*Say* you love me."

"I love you."

"Say it like you mean it."

"I love you, Joe."

Joe lowered his hand. He searched her eyes then took her in his arms. "Oh, darling." He kissed her bloodied face. "I'm so sorry for doubting you. How could I have been so foolish as to believe my mother? She's just trying to break us up, that's what she's trying to do.... Oh, my angel, you're bleeding."

He walked to the washbasin and retrieved the cloth hanging on a rack above it. He dipped the cloth into the water. "But I won't let her," he continued. "No knife can cut our love in two. Angelina, my beautiful angel, please forgive me." Joe bathed her face gently. "I swear it'll never happen again."

"Why do you even want me?" Angelina sobbed. "If I'm stupid and crazy and a Nazi like you always say, why do you even want me?"

"Because I have no choice, darling. You cast your spell and made me fall in love with you. But let's not fight anymore. Let's forget our little spat. Put on that pretty dress I bought you and let's go dancing."

She accepted his olive branch. She was afraid not to.

The morning after Joe left to return to camp, June came to Angelina's door. "If you value your life, I suggest you leave that lunatic."

"Oh, I guess you heard us the other night. I'm so sorry, June."

"What are *you* apologizing for? Yes, I heard every word and every slap. That jackass is going to up and kill you someday. Leave him while you've still got the chance!"

"But how can I leave? Where will I go?"

"Go back home. Tell your folks what he did to you. Look, I'll help you pack. Then we'll take a cab and put you on the train back west."

June's mother came over and watched Timmy while Angelina and June left for the train station. As Angelina boarded the train, June slipped a five-dollar bill in her hand.

"Write me and let me know how you make out," she said.

"WHAT ARE YOU doing here?" Margaretha asked when she saw Angelina walk through the door.

"I've come back home. I've left Joe."

"What! What do you mean? Your place is with your husband, not here."

"But—but, Mama," Angelina sputtered, "He hits me. He insists I cheat on him and he calls me a Nazi. He even tries to make me go to the Catholic church!"

"Well, put away your suitcases then."

Angelina took up where she had left off with her family, and resumed her old chores.

Weeks later when Joe found out through his mother that Angelina was no longer living in the one-room suite, he claimed a family emergency and received a leave. He took a train to Saskatoon then walked out to the farm.

"Why did you leave me?" he asked Angelina when he got there.

"I left because I'm tired of you beating me up. And I'm tired of you always accusing me of cheating on you."

"I know sometimes I lose my temper and I'm sorry, but

I promise things will be different. Here," he said, handing her a bouquet of wildflowers. "I picked these for you. Please, Angelina, my angel, come back home with me."

"I don't want to go back. It isn't just you, it's your folks too."

"We'll move somewhere else, to another city, away from my interfering mother."

"I don't want to go back to you!" Angelina insisted, fleeing up the stairs.

Joe spied Margaretha peeking around the kitchen corner. "Mom, please," he said, his tone ingratiatingly pleading, "may I talk with you?" He stepped into the kitchen. "Look, I don't know what all Angelina's been saying, but I love her."

"She says you beat her."

"I don't beat her. She's exaggerating. We both know she sometimes exaggerates, builds a mountain out of a mole hill," Joe said. "She tells me that Dad used to beat her too and that you let him. I know that can't be true. You never would have let him beat your own daughter; discipline, yes, but not beat. Right?"

"*Ja*, never."

"Well, it is that way with me too. I admit I have slapped her, but only when she deserved it. I found out from my own mother that Angelina cheats on me when I'm away. You know how pretty she is and I'm sure you have seen how men look at her. It is hard, I think, with all that attention, for her to be faithful sometimes. But I truly love her and forgive her and ask only that she return to me. Please talk to her for me, will you?"

Joe walked back to Saskatoon for the night but came back the next morning bearing gifts.

Joe gave a broach to Marie, who was fourteen, and dolls

to Betty, and Rosea. Ernie, eight, received a little toy truck; Baby Ava a rattle. The children were ecstatic about their gifts; such luxuries were hard to come by.

"I'm so happy you like them," Joe said to them. "But I'm not sure if I'll ever see you again. Angelina is breaking up with me." Tears filled his eyes and began dripping down his cheeks. "I love her so much, but she just doesn't seem to love me anymore," he cried.

"Oh, but *we* still like you," Betty said, giving Joe a hug.

"I will talk to Angelina," Marie said. "It's terrible the way she's treating you."

"Thank you, Marie. It's good to know someone still cares for me."

He helped Margaretha repair a few loose boards on the chicken coop.

"Angelina say that you try make her become Catholic," Margaretha said to him.

Joe shook his head. "Angelina has it all wrong. She misunderstands things sometimes. I promised you and Dad that I would not make Angelina join my church and I have not. If I truly wanted to, I could have forced her to change her religion—she is my wife. But I have not and I will not."

Margaretha invited Joe to stay for supper. It was on his lips to accept the offer when he saw Abe coming in from the fields.

"Thank you, Mom, but I must be going. Another time, perhaps."

"Go back to him," Margaretha said to Angelina the next chance she had to be alone with her daughter. "Papa never hits me, and Joe nice to me. Why they only hit you, not me? I think maybe if Joe hit you, you deserve it. Just like Papa sometimes had to hit you. You go back to Joe. Joe is good man. Your place is by your husband, not here."

"I feel sorry for him," Marie said to Angelina, "Can't you see how bad he feels? He even cried. How many men would cry over a woman?"

Angelina went back east with Joe.

12

A YEAR HAD PASSED since Angelina had gone back east with Joe. They had moved to Etobicoke, several miles distant from New Toronto. Angelina now saw less of Joe's folks, though it was still too often for her liking. She had had another miscarriage and Josephine had been belligerent about it.

"I think it just you don't want my Joe's babies," she had said to Angelina.

Now Angelina was again pregnant—this time with twins and in her eighth month. She let herself hope.

It was a hot and humid Ontario night, too hot to remain indoors so Angelina was happy to go along with Joe's suggestion of a walk. Joe took her hand and, in looking like two happy lovers, they began to stroll down the path beside a ravine formed thousands of years earlier by a glacier.

"I love you," Joe murmured.

Angelina didn't echo his words.

Joe asked, "Do you love me?"

Did she love him? No. She had known that even before they married when he had first accused her of cheating on him—and any budding love that may have begun to develop after that had been snuffed out by his behaviour.

"Yes, I love you, Joe," she said dutifully.

They walked a ways in silence.

"You're lying," Joe suddenly declared. "You're lying! I know it!" Joe grabbed Angelina by the hair, forcing her head back. "It's someone else isn't it? Tell me who he is."

"There's no one!"

Joe slapped her. "Tell me!"

Angelina lost her footing. She could feel herself falling—falling down the side of the gorge. Her head struck a rock. She blacked out.

The first thing she noticed when she came to, in the hospital, was that her once hugely rounded belly was now flat.

"My babies, where are my babies?" she screamed.

The attending nun came running. "Quiet down. Quiet down."

"But where are my babies?" Angelina persisted.

"Just settle down and I'll tell you."

Angelina quieted.

"You've been in a coma for a week. During that time you went into labour," the sister said.

"Where are my babies now?" Angelina asked.

"I'm sorry, but they were both stillborn."

Angelina shook her head. "No! No! That can't be. No! I was eight months pregnant. They can't be dead! I felt them moving just the other day. No! You're lying to me. I want my babies!"

"Stop it! I'm not lying to you. Your babies are dead."

"I want to see the doctor. I want to talk to the doctor."

"The doctor is busy right now. He can't talk to you."

"I want to talk to him!"

The nun called for assistance and a large, matronly woman in a nurse's cap and uniform came running. The nurse held Angelina down and the nun injected her with a sedative.

Angelina remained in the hospital for an additional two weeks. During that time she learned that there had been no attending doctor. Her twin boys had been delivered with forceps by the nun.

"What did they look like?" Angelina asked the sister.

"I think it's best if we don't discuss that," she had answered brusquely.

Joe had told the nun that Angelina had slipped, but left out the fact that he had been the cause. Whether or not the woman had believed him, Angelina didn't know. Nor did she care. *If he kills me, fine, then I can finally be done with this world.*

Joe went back to the base shortly after the incident so it was Josephine and Steve who brought Angelina home when it was time for her to be released.

During the ride, Josephine commented, "I no know why they say babies born dead. I see them outside your room when you still sleeping. They in baskets."

"Are you sure, Mom? Are you really sure?"

"Yes, I see them. They alive. They have white hair like you and blue eyes like my Joe's."

The trip home seemed endless. After Steve dropped her off, she went to a neighbour and phoned the base, leaving a message for Joe to call. He did so towards evening. She told him what his mother had said.

There was a pause before he answered. "No, Mom is mistaken. They are not alive."

Years later, Angelina would question why there had been no attending doctor for the delivery and why she had never seen a death certificate, but for the moment her only response was renewed grief.

13

ANGELINA DECIDED TO look for a job. She needed something to take her mind off the loss of her twins.

Surprisingly, Joe was supportive of the idea. "It's just what you need," he said.

Using the certificate for practical nursing she had received in Saskatoon, Angelina found a position in the Mimico Lunatic Asylum as a nurse's aide. Staff turnover was high because working with the insane was hard, often dangerous work. Angelina quickly learned that the stories about events during the full moon were no myth. On that night, extra guards were placed on duty, and additional precautions taken; the lunar cycle really did seem to affect the mood of the patients. The aggressive grew violent and the melancholy even more tearful.

There were underground tunnels that led from one department—they called them cottages—to another. These tunnels were dimly lit and seemed to echo all the patients' moans and screams. Whenever Angelina had to use one of the passages, she always hurried through as quickly as possible.

When she started working there, Angelina set about familiarizing herself with the notes on the patients. The file on the patient in cell 203 caught her attention. Its occupant, Veronica Jones, had once been a professional dancer but had lost her sanity when her lover died.

Rumour had it that she had once had flaming red locks that reached her waist and that she had owned the most beautiful of ballroom gowns. Now her hair was cropped short and her gowns were drab grey. But still, it was said, she sometimes danced.

Angelina kept an eye open every time she passed the woman's room. But night after night the stricken soul just sat there quietly, locked in a world of her own thoughts. Until one evening when Angelina, glancing in the cell, stopped suddenly and stared transfixed as the young woman, clad in her most beautiful attire of all—the bare skin she'd been born in—began to dance. She whirled and swirled, her lovely arched feet seeming to float above the ballroom floor of her cell as she leaped to the symphony God's angels played for her ears alone. Cymbals crashed as the tortuous tempest within her began to rage. Lightning arced, whipping her to and fro. Anguish—cold, and heavy—bent her lithe body. Then, alone and forsaken, beaten, she reached out a quivering hand to the ray of hope heaven offered.

Angelina stood, humbled. She knew she had just been honoured to be the sole audience of one who would forever stand out in her mind as perhaps the most phenomenal dancer who had ever walked this Earth.

THE SORRY STATE in which many of the patients were

kept bothered Angelina deeply. Straitjackets—"packs," as the nurses called them—restrained the more aggressive or uncooperative inmates. The bindings kept their arms rigidly by their sides. If they were itchy, they were unable to scratch themselves. If flies settled on their faces, they had no means to brush them away. Their teeth were brown and stained, and they reeked of body odour. But trying to bathe them was like throwing a cat into a tub. Many of the attendants used brute force and punishment to handle the patients. They hit them with rubber overshoes—it left no marks—or forced them into ice baths.

Angelina's heart went out to these people and she vowed she would do what she could to make their lot a little easier. The first thing she did was buy toothbrushes and scented soaps. She had a calming way with the mentally disturbed. For one thing, she wasn't afraid of them. Asked why this was so, she had replied that it was because she could feel what they felt—trapped and alone—and they could sense her empathy.

Bath time.

"No," patient 27, a husky woman in her thirties, moaned, beast-like.

"Now, Lily," Angelina said imperturbably. "Do you want people to say you stink like a skunk?"

The woman's plain face broke into a sudden smile, and the room filled with the unaccustomed sound of her laughter.

"Yep," Angelina continued, "they'll say, 'That Lily, she smells just like a skunk.'"

More laughter. "No, I don't," she said in a child-like manner.

"Look, Lily. Look at the pretty soap I bought you. Smell it."

Lily took a sniff.

"See? Doesn't that smell nice?"

Lily's eyes widened. She tried to grab the soap.

Angelina evaded her. "Tell you what. If you let me give you a bath, I'll let you keep this pretty soap. Okay?"

Lily nodded.

"You were damn lucky," the nurse Angelina was assisting warned, "I've seen that woman bend a fork with her bare hands. Just keep it in mind that you can never trust any of them."

ANGELINA HAD BEEN working at the asylum for three months when she received a summons from the head matron.

Oh no, she worried. *I'm probably in trouble.* Some of the nurses she worked with didn't approve of her methods of dealing with patients. Had one of them complained?

With trepidation Angelina tapped on the matron's door. She did her best to keep her voice steady. "You wanted to see me, Miss Clark?"

"Yes, come in. Sit down." Miss Clark fingered a pencil. "I've been hearing many stories about you, Angelina. It's been said you give our patients trinkets."

"Yes, ma'am. I give them little things like soap or ribbons for their hair."

"I see. And it's also been brought to my attention that you sometimes interfere with the nurses' attempts to restrain the patients. Why is it that?"

"Ma'am, it's because I try to treat them as *I* would like to be treated if I were in here...ma'am."

Miss Clark raised an eyebrow, took a long, hard look at Angelina, then nodded. "Well, I've also received reports that there have been improvements in many of the patients in your cottage, so I am offering you a higher position. I would like you to teach your methods to the other interns." She paused. "There would, of course, be an increase in pay for you."

Angelina couldn't believe her ears. "Oh, yes," she said. "I would very much like to do that. Thank you, Miss Clark."

But if Angelina thought Joe would be equally impressed, she was wrong.

"So I suppose you think you're some big shot now; that you're better than me because you got a promotion," he groused. "Being able to talk to lunatics doesn't mean you're smart, you know. It just says that you're as crazy as the rest of them."

He harped on the matter for days. Angelina wondered how it was that she could have a calming effect on the mentally ill but had somehow managed to aggravate first her parents, and now her husband.

14

THERE WAS ONE young woman in the asylum whom Angelina's heart went out to especially. The patient, Wilma, had been convicted two years earlier of the gruesome murder of her own mother. But whenever anyone entered her cell, Wilma would scream, "I didn't do it. I didn't do it!" She was usually kept restricted with a pack.

One evening, during the rounds, Angelina asked the accompanying nurse to wait outside Wilma's door, and she entered the cell alone.

Wilma began her usual rant.

"Listen, dear," Angelina said to the bound woman, "when you scream like this it makes people think you're insane. You don't want people to think that, do you?"

"No. But nobody listens. I didn't do it!"

"Well, then you have to tell your story without screaming. If I take off your pack, will you behave and not scream?"

"Yes."

"You promise?"

"Yes. I promise."

Angelina removed the straitjacket. "Now," she said, "tell me your story."

"You really want to hear my story?" the woman asked, surprised.

"Yes. I do."

"No. You won't believe me," Wilma answered, getting agitated again. "No one listens to me."

Angelina knew what that was like. "You know, I have a story to tell, too. If you're willing to listen, I'll tell you mine."

"I'll listen," Wilma said.

"I was about six years old," Angelina began. "My sister, Kathy, who was a year younger than me, and I were playing up in the hayloft. We always had to wear petticoats under our dresses while other girls who weren't of our language could get away with just dresses. We wanted to pretend we were the other girls, the girls we called 'the English.' So we took off our dresses and pranced about in the hayloft in our petticoats. 'Look at me,' we said to each other, 'I'm the *Enjelsch*.'" Angelina's mouth curled up in remembrance. Then she sobered.

"I was having so much fun, I didn't see Peita—he was our fifteen-year old cousin's friend—climbing up the ladder. Kathy did and she tried to warn me, but I didn't hear her. She hid in the hay. Then I turned around and saw him staring at me from the top of the ladder. I quickly scrambled for my dress. I didn't like him very much. He pretended to be nice in front of Mama and Papa, but behind their backs he was mean. One time he stomped on one of our newborn baby kittens and made my sisters and I cry."

"Did you tell your mother and father?" Wilma asked.

"No. We were raised to respect our elders. Besides, we were afraid of him. And now he had caught us with just our petticoats on. If he told Mama, we would be in trouble for sure." Angelina looked at Wilma, whose eyes were steady on her own.

"But as if reading our minds, Peita said, 'Don't worry. I won't tell your Mama what you were doing.' He came closer. He started touching my hair. 'Such a pretty little girl. Give Uncle Peita a kiss.' I was scared. I told him I had to go. He started kissing me. He pushed me back onto the hay. He...he hurt me. What he did to me hurt so bad I couldn't even cry. Then he ran down the steps and out of the barn. I was so sore I could hardly make it down the ladder. I stumbled out of the barn.

"'Mama,' I whimpered, bent over in pain and bleeding. 'Mama!'

"Kathy ran ahead of me, calling towards the house for help. My mother came out.

"'What's wrong?' she asked. She took one look at me, then, holding her hands up in front of her face, she screamed, 'Get away from me, get away!'

"'Mama, help me,' I beseeched.

"'No. No. I don't want to hear it. Go away! Go away!' She covered her ears and ran away from me.

"'Mama!' I screamed again, then collapsed on the ground."

Wilma ground her teeth. "She didn't care! What a horrible mother. Such an evil cousin! Horrible things happen in this world! Horrible! Horrible!" She began rocking herself. "And what happened to you after that? Did he get away with what he did to you?"

"Well, Elsie, an orphan girl who was staying with us at the time, carried me into the house and cleaned me up.

Elsie rocked me and soothed me. She cared for me during the days of my healing. Mama never came near me during that time and I couldn't understand why. Mama never allowed me to talk about what happened. And I don't know what happened to the boy. I never saw him after that and his name was never again spoken of."

Angelina and Wilma sat for a moment in silence. Angelina placed a gentle hand on Wilma's arm. "Tell me, Wilma, what happened to you?"

"I was coming home from a friend's house. I walked in the door and I saw her hitting..." Wilma's voice began to rise. "Hitting my mother with an axe! She hit her and hit her and hit her."

"Okay, dear. Relax. Just take a few deep breaths. That's a girl. Now, who hit her?"

"Flora, my stepfather's girlfriend."

"Your stepfather had a girlfriend?"

"Yes. My real father died when I was a baby. My mother remarried when I was five. Then, a few years ago, I found out my stepfather had a girlfriend. I saw them kissing once in the shadows of the maples. My stepfather asked my mom for a divorce so he could marry Flora. Mom said no."

"So then Flora killed your mother," Angelina stated.

"Yes! She killed my mother!" Flora wailed. "My mother! My mother who used to bake cookies with me, sing to me when I was little, and rock me in her arms. She killed her!"

"All right. Now, I want you tell me what you did when you saw Flora hitting your mother."

"I—I don't remember. At the trial, the police said that my stepfather had called them and that when they arrived I was sitting beside my mother's body with the bloody axe in my hands. I—I guess after I saw Mom, I must have gone into shock or something. When I finally regained some of my senses, I tried to explain the truth but no one would believe me. I'll admit I kind of lost my head after that. It was all too much and they declared me mad. But you've got to believe me, I didn't kill my mother! I didn't!" Her voice trailed off into the beginning of a wail.

Angelina's tone was a soothing balm. "I believe you, Wilma. And I'm going to talk to the head matron for you. Now, if she asks to speak to you, explain your story just the way you did to me, slowly and calmly, okay? I won't put you back in the pack, but remember—no screaming."

Wilma took Angelina's advice and no longer ranted when staff entered her room. Angelina brought the woman's case to Miss Clark, who promised to look into it.

ANGELINA HAD BEEN working at the hospital for a year when she once again found herself pregnant. Considering that and the fact Joe continued to harp about her job, she thought it was best if she resign.

"I'm sorry to see you go, Angelina. We're going to miss you. Should you ever decide to come back, you can be assured that there will be position for you," Miss Clark promised.

Angelina never did learn whether Wilma was acquitted or not.

On Angelina's last day of work Joe came to pick her up, waiting for her outside on a bench in the grounds. It was the first time he had ever sat there. A few low-risk patients were outside working on the flowerbeds. One of them had turned his wheelbarrow upside down. Joe asked the man why he had it sitting like that.

"You think I'm crazy?" the inmate answered him. "If I

put it the right way, they'll fill it up and I'll have to empty it again."

Joe found the man's words hilarious and he told all his friends at the Legion about it.

"Nope, I'm not so crazy as to put my wheelbarrow right-side up!"

15

On July 29, 1946, Angelina gave birth to a little boy, Danny. He was perfect. Angelina knew; she had checked every inch of him.

"Look at his slender fingers," she commented to Joe, "he'll be able to play a piano for sure."

Angelina and Joe both agreed that Danny, with his dark brown curls, sapphire-blue eyes and cupid's bow lips, was undeniably the most beautiful baby ever born.

Angelina's only regret was that she was unable to breastfeed. Because of complications during Danny's birth, she had been too weak to hold and nurse him. By the time Angelina was stronger, Danny had already adopted the bottle.

Angelina was determined to be the perfect mother. Danny was fed every four hours, exactly to the minute. Nothing that touched his little hands and mouth were not first sterilized. He never had to lie in a wet, soggy diaper.

"No one, not even the angels in heaven, can take better care of my baby!" Angelina vowed.

Joe was equally enthralled by his new son. When they went out in public, he insisted on being the one to carry and show off the baby. And in the evenings, it was Joe who bathed and dressed him.

The war was over, but the planes were still kept in readiness. Advanced training in their servicing was being taught in Saskatoon. Joe applied for the course.

"You know," he said to Angelina, "I think it's time we put some distance between us and my interfering mother."

Joe's application was accepted. He bought a couple of lots on the outskirts of Saskatoon about four blocks from Angelina's family, and then he and Angelina proceeded to build a small house in their spare time. They soon realized that they worked well together. Both of them held the opinion that whatever job you tackled, it should be done right.

For once life was good. Joe was happy. Angelina was happy. She even began to think that perhaps she did love Joe after all.

Danny was five and a half months old the morning Angelina walked into his room; the morning she lifted his cold, still body out of his crib and then dropped it back down, screaming "No. No!"; the morning she ran the quarter-mile barefoot, clad only in her nightgown, through snow to get to her Mama and Papa's house for help.

"Danny's dead! Danny's dead!" she cried, running through the door.

"Dead? What?" Abe asked, unbelieving.

"My baby's dead!"

"No, it can't be." Margaretha said.

"He's cold. He's blue. He's not moving. He...he is—is... dead!" Angelina uttered the last word in a wail.

"Where is he now? Where is Joe?" Abe wanted to know.

"At the house."

"You stay here." Abe threw on his coat and raced out the door.

"Mama," Angelina, moaned, "my baby's dead. My baby's dead."

"Maybe not. Maybe you just think so. Papa will see. Let's read the Bible together and pray," Margaretha suggested.

Abe found Joe desperately rubbing his son's little body and holding him above the fireplace.

"Danny is cold. I have to warm him up," Joe said in a daze.

Abe had been a farmer all his life and one look at his grandson told him Danny would never be warm again.

"Son," he said, "We go now, you, me, baby to my house. We get doctor."

The doctor came. Joe cried. Angelina cried. Margaretha took Angelina in her arms and for the first time that Angelina could remember, rocked her.

"I know it hurts, my *kjleenet Kjint,* I know," Margaretha lulled, and she did know. Just months before, she too had lost an infant son. Leonard, her baby, had ingested glass that had been accidentally ground into the baby cereal in the factory where it had been produced.

In that moment of pain, mother and daughter shared a common bond, and somewhere through the dark abyss a thought flashed through Angelina's mind. *Maybe Mama does love me a little bit after all.*

The coroner called it crib death—sudden infant death syndrome. The doctor said it wasn't known why, but that sometimes a baby just went to sleep and never woke up again.

Angelina was inconsolable, she blamed herself—why hadn't she woken sooner? Had he cried out and she not heard him? Or was it the proud words she had uttered months earlier, that even the angels in heaven could not take better care of her baby than she could? Yes, maybe that was it. God was showing her!

Joe took to drinking and once again slapped his wife around. "It's your fault," he accused Angelina. "You slept through our baby dying!"

When Danny was a few weeks old Angelina had agreed to let Joe have him baptized into the Catholic Church. Then, after he died, a Mass was held for him in St. Joseph's Cathedral in Saskatoon, presided over by Father O'Brien. During the following weeks, Father O'Brien came to the house frequently, offering comfort and support to Joe and Angelina. One day, alone with the priest, Angelina asked the kindly man for advice.

"What can I do?" Angelina pleaded. "Joe goes straight to the hotel after work to drink and when he comes home he hits me. He says it's my fault Danny died. He says that if I had been a Catholic, it wouldn't have happened."

"My dear, like you, Joe is grieving. He's not thinking straight. I'm sure he doesn't really mean the things he's saying. But mixed marriages between two different faiths can be trying at the best of times. Are you firm in your Mennonite faith, do you go to the services frequently?"

"No. Except for weddings and a funeral in my family, I haven't been to church since I married Joe."

"Can I make a suggestion?"

"By all means, please."

"You could be baptized into the Church. Retain your own beliefs. What you believe is private anyway, between you and God. But joining the Catholic Church may ease some of the tension between you and your husband."

Angelina followed Father O'Brien's suggestion.

Around the same time that Angelina was baptized into Catholicism, Abe and Margaretha also changed religions. They became Pentecostals. "Pentecostals are more happy in their worship," they said.

At the end of Joe's course, he announced, "We're moving back to Ontario. I'm tired of this godforsaken prairie and drought, and..." he didn't finish his sentence but Angelina knew he had been about to say "and death."

16

ANGELINA WAS WALKING down the road to nowhere.

Two nights earlier, she and Joe had been sitting on the sofa together in their apartment listening to the radio when Joe suddenly slammed down his drink.

What's the matter now? Angelina had wondered. "What's wrong?" she asked aloud.

"You know damn well what's wrong," her husband had growled.

"No, I don't," Angelina protested.

"You're a two-timing whore."

"Not this again!" Angelina exclaimed.

"Don't put on the innocent mask for me! You, just sitting there looking all innocent while you're cheating on me in your mind. I know you; I know how you think! It's written all over your face. You're envisioning sex with your Prince Charming."

Angelina's traitorous face shaded to red. Joe was right; she *had* been daydreaming about a man, but he had the details all wrong. In her fantasy, she had met a kind, gentle man, who whisked her away from her miserable life with Joe. But there had been no sex, just a petal-soft kiss.

"I knew it!" Joe exclaimed in triumph. "Who is he? Someone at the Legion? The milkman?"

"No, he isn't anyone!"

"You're lying! You're always lying to me! Tell me who he is!" Joe demanded. He began twisting Angelina's arm. "Tell me!"

Angelina screamed. There was an audible snap. Angelina blacked out.

"Angelina, Angelina," Joe was shaking her. "Wake up."

"My arm," Angelina moaned. "My arm!" she cried.

"Well, I hope it's broken, after what you did to me. You deserve it. I hope you have some blue marks. You do look *so* beautiful in blue."

"Please, Joe, I think my arm is broken," Angelina sobbed.

"All right, all right, I'll take you to the hospital."

"What happened?" the doctor asked the couple when they walked in.

"She fell down the steps," Joe answered for Angelina. "My poor wife can be so clumsy sometimes."

The break didn't look like the result of a fall. "Is that what happened, Mrs. Jaslo?" the doctor asked.

Angelina evaded his eyes. "Yes," she answered.

The doctor sighed. Without another word he set the break.

After that she slipped into a sort of stupor. Joe brought her home, he tried to get her to eat, she heard him apologize but it was as though she were viewing it all from a distance, as though it were all happening to someone else.

Then, today, she suddenly woke to find herself back in her body and walking down the highway.

She wished she could have just stayed gone. *I hope someone runs me over. What do I have to live for anyway? My baby is dead. I want to be dead, too.*

She walked a couple of miles down the black asphalt, lost in her torment. She had been faithful to Joe, damn it; not once had she cheated on him. Not that it had been from lack of opportunity. Men seemed to find her attractive, though why she couldn't at all understand—her nose was too big and her mother-in-law said she had a head shaped like a pig's. Joe, however, had not been faithful to her, she knew. He had affairs. On one occasion, he had even brought the woman home with him and slept with her on the sofa. Angelina hadn't minded—at least that night Joe had left her alone. The only thing she had said afterwards was, "You keep accusing me of cheating, but you're the one who's doing it."

"That's different," he had returned "I'm a man, I'm allowed that."

SEVERAL MOTORISTS STOPPED to offer Angelina a ride, but she waved them on. A fourteen-wheeler appeared in the near distance. She stuck out her thumb.

The driver stopped. "Where are you heading?" he asked.

Where am I heading? "To Sudbury, to visit my sister." It just came out of her mouth.

"Hop in."

He's got sad eyes. That was her first impression of the trucker. She took in his lumberman's jacket with the rolled-up sleeves. He looked to be in his early thirties with slightly-receding, dusty-blond hair, an average looking kind of guy.

I can trust this man, was Angelina's gut feeling.

"Thank you for stopping, Mr.—?"

"Mike."

"Thank you for stopping, Mike. I'm Angelina. Have you come a long way?" she asked.

"I'm hauling from Indiana."

"Oh, that's a fair ways."

They sat in silence for a few minutes.

"You must get lonely," she said.

"Yeah. Well. You get used to it after awhile."

"Are you married, Mike?"

"I was."

"Do you mind if I ask what happened?"

"She left me."

"Did you hit her? Is that why she left?"

"No. I don't do that kind of thing."

"Why, then, did she leave?"

"She found another man. He had more money than I did. A better job. He could buy her things I couldn't."

Angelina waited until she was sure he had finished his outpouring before asking, "Did she say that's why she left?"

"No. She didn't need to. He's a lawyer. She's used to money. Her dad's a doctor."

"That's not a good reason to leave. I'm so sorry, Mike." She reached over and touched his arm.

"Yeah. Well. That's life, I guess. What happened to your arm?" he asked.

But Angelina wasn't yet ready to share her own truth. "Oh…I fell down the steps yesterday. I stumbled over the ledge while I went for the morning paper."

She was ashamed to admit to him that she was the type of woman who would tolerate a man who beat her. She was humiliated that her neighbours knew.

Mr. and Mrs. Johnson next door had said, "We know

you're not having a good life with your husband. We pray for you every night."

Mrs. Smith from across the street said, "I know how he treats you. Why do you put up with it? I'd never stick around if my husband did that to me. I can't for the world of me understand why you stay."

But what could Angelina say when she herself didn't know the answer?

By the time they reached Sudbury, Angelina had learned that Mike had a sister and brother to whom he was very close, had been raised near Nelson, B.C. and chosen a career driving semi trailers because he liked to see the country. She also discovered he had a soft spot for kids, liked dogs, and had once had a teddy bear named Lion.

When they reached Sudbury, Mike asked Angelina for her sister's address.

"Oh, don't bother driving me all the way there. Just drop me off at this coffee shop here."

Mike looked at her. "There is no sister, is there? And I'm not buying your 'falling down the steps' story, Angelina." He took her good hand. "You're much too good a woman for that, you know."

"I'm too good a woman to fall down the steps, Mike?" Angelina tried to tease through a sudden mist of tears.

"Your old man broke your arm, didn't he?"

Though she had removed her ring, he could still see the white outline on her finger.

Angelina looked down, ashamed.

"Come with me to my place. I might not have much, but I'd treat you right."

"I can't, Mike."

Mike drove to a motel and rented a room for her.

A sudden thought came to Angelina. *If he's going to keep*

accusing me of it, why not do it? Yes. Since Joe kept calling her a slut...well, then, she was going to be one. That night, she and Mike shared the room and found mutual comfort in each other's arms.

In the morning, Mike asked, "Won't you reconsider my offer?"

"I'm sorry, Mike, but I just can't. Don't worry about me. I'll be all right."

Their paths never crossed again.

Angelina hitched a different ride back home, expecting another beating when she walked in the door, but Joe surprised her.

"Oh, honey," he said. "I'm so glad to see you home. I've missed you so much." He took her in his arms. "Oh, Angelina, you are so beautiful." He kissed her tenderly. "You know? We should go dancing this weekend."

"How can I go dancing with my arm in a cast?" Angelina retorted.

"Oh," Joe looked down, properly chagrined. "Oh, honey, I'm so sorry for what I did. It's just that you're so beautiful. I know men can't keep their eyes off you and the thought of losing you kills me. But I'll be different, I promise."

And he was. The honeymoon lasted three months, until he came home one night drunk and beat Angelina once again.

A pattern began to emerge that lasted for years. Joe would hit Angelina and she would run away for a couple of days, seeking vindication through a one-night stand. When asked years later by a counsellor if she had ever told Joe what she had been doing, she said she hadn't, and, giving it some thought, came to the realization that what she had done had not hurt him at all. She had succeeded only in becoming the whore Joe had accused her of being.

17

DEAR ANGELINA,

How are you? I'm fine, I guess. I was just wondering if I could get your help. I'm expecting another baby soon. Bob is out in B.C., working. I was wondering if you could come on out to the farm and stay with me until after the baby is born. I'm going to have it at home—the hospital is too far away. The doctor said that he will come here to deliver it.

I know it's a long way, but please try to come, okay? If you do, just go see my brother-in-law, Anton. He's got a shoe shop in Turtleford. He'll tell you how to get to my place.

Sis Marie

MARIE'S HEALTH WAS delicate. And now she was having a second child when her first was only nine-and-a-half months old.

When Angelina told Joe about the letter, he said, "No you're not going."

She didn't argue.

Early the next morning, after Joe left for work, she packed her suitcases. *My sister needs me.* She took a taxi to the train station and bought a ticket to Saskatoon.

Once in Saskatoon, she would spend a night with her folks before boarding the day train to Turtleford, a small town about a hundred and fifty miles northeast of the city.

Joe would figure out she had left to be with her sister, but it was doubtful he would pursue her. He had grown accustomed to her coming and going, and he had a good job he enjoyed, working once again as an airframe mechanic at a base in Erin Ferry. It was unlikely he would jeopardize his position by going off on a tangent.

Angelina boarded the train and handed the conductor her ticket, then settled back for the two-day journey ahead of her. She thought about her sister Marie, whom she hadn't seen for ages.

Marie and their younger sister, Betty, had taken a trip out to Vancouver a few years earlier. While there, Marie had met and married a fisherman. The irony of it was that the man turned out to be one of her people—Dutch Mennonite. Marie had always said that one day she would move far away from "boring Saskatchewan" and marry one of the *Enjelsch*. And here she had gone all the way to Vancouver just to end up with someone of her own background anyway.

Angelina wondered how Marie's health was holding out. She had always been the sickly one in the family. It had been years before the doctors had finally ascertained that she had asthma. Because of her poor health she had gotten away with much more than her siblings did. When she worked, she often started wheezing and Mama would tell the other girls—Angelina, Kathy, or Betty—to take over the chore for Marie.

Angelina and Kathy, being the oldest, were expected to help care for the younger ones. Sometimes Marie seemed to delight in getting them into trouble.

"What do you mean, you can't find her gloves?" Mama asked them one time. "I've told you to always put them in one spot when you take them off her hands. Why must I always tell you girls everything?"

The next day at school, Marie had laughed about it. "Hee, hee, hee! I sure played a good one on all of you. I hid them."

Angelina and Kathy had been angry but they knew there was little they could do but scold. Marie would tattle.

Whenever Papa had attempted to punish Marie for a misdemeanour, Mama would stop him. "But, Abe, she's sick," she would say.

The times Papa did manage to spank Marie, she would taunt, "You think that hurt?"

Unable to break her and knowing Mama's protective feelings for her, he usually gave up in defeat.

Until the last time.

The last time, according to Kathy, had been a couple of years after Angelina had married. Marie had angered Papa for some reason or another, and he had horsewhipped her until the blood flowed. Mama wasn't home and Kathy, terrified he would kill Marie, ran to a neighbour for help. Papa was arrested. Papa promised the judge that he would never beat his children again. He was released. The kids still at home said that Papa had kept his word.

Marie would be twenty now. Kathy was twenty-two and married. Mama had informed her by letter that her sister Rosea had recently married as well. *Hee S Rush,* ("he is Russian") she had written. Actually, he was from the Ukraine, but in Mama's eyes, he was *Rush.*

When Angelina arrived in Saskatoon, her father was waiting for her at the train station. "Oh, my Angelina," he said, giving her a big bear hug. "How I've missed you!"

"I've missed you too, Papa. How are Mama and Ernie and the kids?"

"They are all fine and anxious to see you again."

"How are you keeping yourself, Papa?"

"Oh, I am fine."

"I hear you work for the city now."

"Yes."

Her mother had told her that in one of her letters. Papa was what the English called "the honey man." It was his job to shovel the waste from the privy traps into the waiting box of a city truck.

Angelina could see the humiliation in her father's eyes. "You are a hard worker, Papa," she said, "there is no shame in that."

"So are you, my *kjleenet Kjint.* When you were at home, I didn't see how hard you did work. I am sorry for that. So much I am sorry for."

When Angelina walked through the door, her mother asked, "Have you just come to help out Marie or have you left your husband again too?"

"No," Angelina replied, "I've just come to help Marie."

"Goot," Margaretha said.

A girl with a ponytail dragging a little boy by the hand came running up to her.

"Ava, is that you?" Angelina exclaimed.

"Yes," the girl said, running into Angelina's open arms. "It's me."

"Oh, my little Avie, it's so good to see you again! I was worried you wouldn't remember me. You were only five when I last saw you."

"I could never forget you. You're my sister but you always feel more like an aunty to me. I remember the things you did with me when you lived close by, like showing me how to make necklaces out of dandelions."

They hugged, then Ava shoved her little brother at Angelina. "This is your sister, Angelina," she said to him.

"Ike?" Angelina asked incredulously. "But, my how you have grown! You both have." The last time she had seen her baby brother he had still been in diapers.

"Ike, give your sister a hug," Ava ordered.

"No. I don't know her. She isn't my sister," Ike proclaimed.

"Yes, she is," Ava insisted.

"No, she ain't. I never seen her before."

"She is your sister," Ava said. "Hug her."

"No. Don't wanna." He set his jaw and crossed his arms.

Mama and Papa have changed. If I had said something like that to one of my elders when I was a child, I would have got it on the "moozh noaktijch."

A boy in his early teens came into the kitchen where Angelina was standing. "Hi, sis," he said.

"Ernie!" Angelina cried. She embraced her brother tightly. "It's so good to see you again."

Ernie tapped her on her back in return. Though happy to see her, he was now "too old" for such open gestures of affection.

Angelina held her brother out in front of her to get a better look at him.

He stood a good six inches taller than she did and sported heavy muscle, honestly earned. He had been helping out his father after school and during holidays almost since the day he had started walking. To Abe, work was everything and he often pushed Ernie hard. One of the boy's jobs had been to harness the horses. Ernie had grown to hate horses and vowed that when he had a place of his own there would not be even one horse on it. And work for Ernie hadn't ended when Abe took on employment with the city. To earn extra income, Abe and Ernie also searched for and brought copper and other scrap metal in to salvaging companies, and they sourced firewood and manure to sell.

"Come sit," Margaretha said to Angelina. "I have made you a lunch."

She set a plate of fried Mennonite sausage and small, unpeeled boiled potatoes in front of her daughter.

"Oh, Mama, you remembered!" Angelina said in delight. "You remembered that I like potatoes with the skins on."

"How could I forget? When you were little, we would go visiting at your Grosma Bickert's house. You would crawl up on her lap and she would give you pieces of cooked potato to eat and you would be so happy. Sometimes I used to think that you liked her more than you liked me."

"Oh, Mama, I love you too," Angelina insisted, giving her mother a big hug. "It's just that Grosma Bickert was more like me. You are more like your mama, Grosma Ginter, was."

Many in the family had not much cared for Abe's mother; they called her a lazy *Rushlander*, a sloppy housekeeper. Unlike Rosea Ginter, who had been born in Canada, Agathena Bickert had been born in Russia and had emigrated to Canada with a later wave of Mennonites. The villagers had whispered that she was a witch. She saw things before they happened and communicated with the dead.

"How," Angelina had once asked her grandmother, "do you know when someone has died?"

"A wavy, foggy thing—*en jeist*—comes and tells me. Your father always knew too. But it was birds that told him. But now he says it isn't so. I know he says that because he is afraid that God will strike him dead. You too are like me. You are different than most people. I saw it the moment I first held you in my arms."

Angelina had adored her Grosma. On long, cold winter days, Angelina could often be seen sitting by her grandmother's side, helping her strip the down off chicken feathers, which they had collected throughout the year. Most couldn't be bothered, for it was slow, tedious work—not at all like collecting the down from geese. But Agathena had done it and used the down to make comforters for her family and pillows to trade, come spring, at the market in Saskatoon for rich soil for her boxes. Agathena planted everything from flowers to vegetables in wooden boxes.

"They all think I'm lazy and that I'm crazy," she told Angelina one day. "But just you wait, it will be me laughing when they have all the weeds to pick and I have none."

It was true. Everyone admitted that though Agathena Bickert was crazy, she did keep beautiful gardens.

"Yes," Angelina's mother now said, "You did inherit many of your Grosma's ways."

After lunch, Angelina visited with the family for a bit before retiring for the night. She was tired; she hadn't been able to afford a berth on the train.

The next afternoon found Angelina stepping off the bus she had taken to Turtleford. Upon receiving directions to the shoe shop, she collected her suitcases and began crossing the street, trudging through the April mud and sludge. *I'm glad I brought my boots.*

Seeing her struggle, a young man asked, "Do you need help, ma'am?"

"Oh, thank you," Angelina answered as he took the cases from her. "I'm just heading to the shoe shop. My sister's brother-in-law works there."

"That would be Anton Wiebe." The gentleman walked with her to the shop. He deposited her luggage inside the doorway and called out, "Anton, there is a lady here to see you."

A lanky, silvery-blond haired man looking to be in his early twenties came out of a back room.

"May I help you?" he inquired.

"I am Angelina Jaslo, Marie's sister." She stuck out her hand.

He accepted it with a genial smile. "Pleased to meet you, Mrs. Jaslo."

"I've come to see Marie. I was wondering if you could give me directions to her house."

"Well, if you don't mind waiting for a bit, I'll walk you out there."

"Oh, I couldn't impose."

"It's no imposition. I'm going there today anyway. I'm staying out at the house to help with the wood and such while Bob is gone."

Half an hour later, Mr. Wiebe closed the shop for the day. He picked up Angelina's two suitcases. "It's about two miles from here."

"Thank you," Angelina said with a smile. "How is Marie doing?"

"Oh, she's holding out pretty good. She's a little tired sometimes."

"So your brother is working in B.C.?" Angelina confirmed.

"Yes, he's fishing out by Vancouver but he's due back in another month or so."

The couple's booted feet tromped alternately through

puddles of slush and mounds of packed prairie snow as they climbed up one side of a brush-studded hill and down another. The April wind had a cool edge to it and Angelina buttoned up her wool coat. *I could sure use a cup of tea when I get there. I'd even settle for coffee.*

"Are you originally from around here, Mr. Wiebe?"

"Please, call me Anton. And, no. I was born in Laird, forty miles north of Saskatoon, but a few years ago, Bob and I got itchy feet and decided we wanted to see Vancouver. We joined a fishing boat. Bob took to the sea right away, though I didn't much care for it myself. Then Bob met Marie and got married. After awhile, she got homesick for Saskatchewan so we all moved back."

"So how did you all end up in Turtleford?"

"Well, I learned the trade of shoemaking from my father, who has his own shop in Laird. When we got back from B.C. I heard that a shoe repair shop in Turtleford was up for sale, so I inquired and bought the place. Bob and Marie followed me out. Bob worked as my assistant for awhile but he missed the big bucks he made at the Coast, so he went back to fishing seasonally."

"And who is older, you or Bob?"

"Bob is older than me by two years."

A cream-coloured cottage came into view.

Angelina followed Anton through the door, a porch, and into the kitchen.

"Marie, I brought someone home for you," Anton hollered out.

Angelina heard the sound of scuffling feet coming from another room. Her sister came into view.

"Sis! You came!" Marie exclaimed happily. Her flaxen curls bounced in exuberance.

"Oh, Marie, it's so good to see you again! I've missed you so much!" Angelina hurried to hug and kiss her sister.

Marie allowed the embrace for a few seconds, patting Angelina in a staccato on the back before pulling away.

She still doesn't like to hug—just like Mama.

"Hi," came another voice.

"Betty, you're here too?" Angelina asked, surprised and delighted to see yet another sister. "Last I heard, you were working on a farm somewhere."

"I moved out to Turtleford about a month ago. I'm working as a waitress in town."

"Oh, this is wonderful!" Angelina squealed. "It's going to be like a sister reunion!" She gave Betty, who responded in the same manner Marie had, a hug as well.

While still living at home, Angelina had been second mother to Betty—Kathy had been responsible for the younger Rosea. Betty's health had been fairly good, though she suffered from occasional fainting spells. She would suddenly pass out, then come to just as quickly.

Betty had idolized Angelina and followed her about like a puppy. Sometimes it had gotten a little annoying, especially on the occasions Angelina and Kathy tried to sneak away from the farm for a bit. One evening when Betty had been nine or ten, Angelina and Kathy slipped away to go to meet some friends in town. They were planning to see a movie. Unbeknownst to either of them, Betty had followed them to town at a distance. They boarded the streetcar and it wasn't until they reached their destination that they realized Betty was aboard also. Angelina and Kathy told Betty she had to go back home, and then stepped down from the car. They had walked but a few feet when they heard a commotion. Concerned about Betty, Angelina ran back to the trolley. Betty was lying motionless on the floor.

She came to within a few minutes, but Angelina told Kathy to go on ahead to the movie without her and accompanied Betty home. After that, it seemed to Angelina, their relationship changed. Betty grew distant, as though resentful of Angelina for having deserted her that night.

Maybe now, Angelina hoped, they would have the chance to rekindle the closeness they had once enjoyed.

"Well, actually I live in town with a girlfriend of mine," Betty answered. "I'm just here for the day, visiting. I'm heading back early tomorrow morning."

Angelina felt a twinge of disappointment.

"Don't worry, she'll be back. She misses me too much," Marie said.

Angelina was a little surprised. During their days at home, Marie and Betty had not gotten along that well. Betty had resented her mother's leniency towards Marie—Betty was a year and a half younger, yet she often ended up having to do Marie's chores for her. And now here Betty had not only gone to Vancouver with Marie but now lived near her as well.

That's good. I guess they have learned how to get along.

"Excuse the mess. I've just been too tired to clean. Here, come sit." Marie waddled on her two swollen legs, making a path through mounds of dirty clothes strewn on the floor. The smell of soiled diapers permeated the air. Marie cleared a basin of unwashed dishes off a cot, which served as a sofa, in the living room.

Angelina sat.

"Where's your baby? Mama said it's a girl?"

"Yeah, a girl. Mandy. She's sleeping. She'll probably be awake pretty soon, though." Addressing her younger sister, Marie said, "Betty, go get the coffee pot, would you?" Then, turning her attention back to Angelina she asked, "So tell me. How have you been?"

"Oh, not too bad."

"How are Mom and Dad and the kids?"

"They're all doing fine."

"From what I've seen, Dad spoils Ava and Ike rotten. It sure wasn't like that for us, eh?" Marie grabbed two dirty cups out of the dish basin and gave them a couple of quick swipes with a grimy dishcloth.

Betty began pouring the coffee.

"Oh, thank you, but none for me," Angelina said.

IT WAS NINE in the morning. Angelina lay in bed thinking about the previous night. She and her sisters had chatted into the wee hours, reminiscing.

"Remember that time Taunte Sosche pulled that good one on Papa?" Angelina had asked.

"Which one?" Marie had queried. Their aunt—their mother's sister—and father often played pranks on each other.

"The hot pepper time."

"The hot pepper time?" Betty echoed, confused.

"Oh, yeah! I'd forgotten about that one!" Marie said. She recalled the story for Betty.

"Dad had had the habit, when he needed to use the outhouse, of announcing it several times before he actually went out. Then one time, at his first announcement, Taunte Sosche, winking at Mom, quickly sneaked outside. 'Yep, I better get on out there,' Dad was saying yet again when Taunte Sosche walked back in. He went out. A few minutes later he came running back through the door. 'Yow! Yow!' he howled in pain. Taunte Sosche giggled. Dad looked at her and knew she was the one to blame. 'I'm gonna get you, Sosche,' he yelled. Taunte Sosche took off streaking though the house, laughing her head off. We learned later that she had replaced the catalogue out in the outhouse with squares cut from a hot pepper sack." Marie giggled. "Dad never again went broadcasting when he had to go!"

"You know, if we had ever tried to pull a stunt like that, or went running through the house like that, we would have got the beating of our lives," Angelina reflected. "But Papa tolerated anything from Taunte Sosche. You know, sometimes I used to wonder if maybe he wished he could have married her instead of Mama."

How good it had felt to talk to her sisters. The three of them had laughed until the tears flowed. Angelina stretched and got out of bed—Anton's bed. He had given it up for her and Betty and slept on the cot. The house was quiet. Marie had been up with the baby sometime earlier, but now they were both asleep. Anton and Betty had left for Turtleford hours ago.

Angelina dressed and then set to work. She added a few more sticks of wood to the stove and began heating a basin of water. When the water was hot, she pulled it over to a cooler spot, filled it with dishes and began washing. She disliked the chore at home—it was one of those 'have to's'—but at other people's houses she didn't mind the job. Once the dishes were washed, she gathered the dirty clothes strewn about into a pile and began sweeping the floor.

After tidying up the house, Angelina made tea and some breakfast for herself. As she had the previous evening, she seated herself on the cot in the living room.

What Marie needs is a table and chairs.

Angelina had noticed a heap of what looked like furniture beside the house yesterday when she had first arrived.

When she had time, she would look through it. Today the dirty laundry must be her priority.

Breakfast finished, Angelina got up and began heating water on the stove again, this time to pour into the wringer-washer.

Marie walked groggily into the kitchen. Mandy, hungry, had woken her.

"Good morning, sis," Angelina said merrily.

"Morning," Marie responded, omitting the "good."

Angelina continued smiling. Mama had always been grouchy in the morning too, and Angelina had vowed that when she herself was an adult she would always try to act cheerful in the morning regardless of how tired she might be.

"I'll make you and Mandy some breakfast," she said. "Do you still like your eggs sunny-side up?"

"That's okay, sis; I just want coffee."

Angelina picked up the percolator that was keeping warm on the back of the stove.

Oh, my gosh, it's grimy. I'm going to have to give it a good cleaning. She handed Marie a cup of coffee. *I wonder if Marie is going to notice all I've done.*

It took a bit of time, but Marie finally said, "Oh, you did the dishes. Thanks."

IT WAS ANGELINA'S third day there before she had a chance to look at the mound outside. She found a conglomeration of kitchen tabletops and stands, and chairs with broken or missing legs and backs sticking out of a drift of the remaining snow against the side of the house.

Maybe I can make something out of all this.

Angelina tugged on a leg; the wooden table it was attached to didn't budge. *It's frozen into the snow.* She went in search of a shovel and found one in the shed. After much hacking, digging, and tugging, she managed to pull the table out of the snow hill. She looked it over critically. One of its square legs was broken. The top had a few scratches but other than that, it seemed to be in fairly good condition. She yanked out the other table. Its arborite surface was cracked and peeling, but its metal legs were still in good shape. She went back into the house.

Marie was feeding Mandy mashed vegetables mixed with potatoes and gravy. Mandy was a cherub with blue eyes and tight, flaxen curls.

She's a living doll, thought Angelina. *If my twins had lived they might have looked like her.*

"Do you have string, sis?" Angelina asked Marie.

"Yeah, there's probably some around here somewhere. What do you need string for?"

"I want to measure something."

"Oh. Well you can look in the drawers, there might be some."

After a few minutes of unsuccessful rummaging, Angelina went to her suitcase and pulled out her housecoat. It had a long belt. *This will do just fine.* She went back outside. She ran the sash down the leg of one table, pinched its length, and compared its measurement with the leg on the other table.

It'll work. Now to get that bad leg off. It was nailed to the inner corner of the table. *I need a hammer.*

She searched in the shed. No luck. She went back into the house.

"Sis, do you have a hammer?"

"I don't know." Marie was holding Mandy on her hip and sipping from a cup of coffee. A cigarette burned in the ashtray on the stove's water reservoir, close to hand.

Angelina went searching in the cellar, but other than canning jars and spider webs, it was empty. She went back upstairs.

Marie was looking at a picture in an Eaton's catalogue. "When Bob gets back with some money, I'm going to get my hair set up into waves like Betty Grable's." She tossed her long, pale-blond tresses out of her eyes. "Her hairdo is so keen, don't you think? And I'm going to buy a pair of nylons and a new garter, and a pretty dress and go to a spiffy restaurant. You should have seen all the fancy restaurants they have in Vancouver."

"They have some pretty nice ones in Toronto too," Angelina replied, looking through the kitchen drawers. "You know, maybe sometime I could cut your hair and set it for you, if you like."

"Oh, would you?" Marie exclaimed.

Angelina finally spotted a hammer high on a shelf in the porch. Its handle had cracked off near the middle.

This will have to do.

She went back outside and tried prying loose the nails holding the broken table leg in place. But the claw was unable to get a grip on them. Angelina hammered down the wood in an attempt to separate it from the nails. It budged a fraction. She hammered, tugged, and hammered some more until she was finally able to pry the nails out. Then she went in search of a screwdriver to remove the screws securing the metal legs to the other table. She finally settled for a butter knife.

To mount the metal plate and leg onto the good table she would first have to glue a small block of wood to its underside. Flour glue wouldn't have a strong enough bond. For this job she needed wood glue.

"Need a hand?" a voice behind her said.

Angelina spun around. It was Anton. "Oh, you scared me," she said. "I thought you would still be at your shop."

"I close up early on Saturday. What are you doing?"

"I'm trying to make a table out of these broken ones. But I need wood glue," she answered.

"It looks like you could use a decent hammer too."

"Yes, and a screwdriver, and a hand saw."

Anton promised Angelina that he would get the tools and glue she needed on Monday.

Sure enough, two days later, he trudged home after work with the supplies.

"I'll give you a hand," he offered.

By evening they had a serviceable table.

"We did it!" Angelina said.

"Yes, we did." Anton looked at her in admiration. "What made you think of doing that in the first place?"

"My mother. We moved a lot, following Papa from job to job. I remember, Mama and I would just get a place looking nice and then we'd have to move again."

"Maybe we could make some usable chairs out of all this junk too."

"Yes, I think we could, but let's keep it a surprise until we're all done. Okay?"

"Okay. Same time tomorrow?" Anton said, grinning.

"Yep."

Angelina followed him into the house and prepared a cup of tea for herself.

"What have you guys been doing out there?" Marie asked, looking up from the Harlequin romance she was reading.

"Oh, a little of this and a little of that." Angelina said.

During the next two days, Angelina and Anton made three functional chairs.

"A table and chairs," Marie commented when they brought them in, "Where did you get those?"

"Anton and I made them," Angelina stated proudly.

"Swell," Marie said.

Angelina was disappointed—she had hoped her sister would say more than that.

Angelina took it a step further with Betty. When next her sister came to visit, she said, "Look what Anton and I made. I think we did a pretty good job, don't you?"

"Looks okay, but you really didn't have to. We were getting along fine without a table and chairs."

Marie said nothing.

Anton merely exchanged looks with Angelina and shrugged, but Angelina was disenchanted. *We worked hard to fix that furniture and here they don't even appreciate it.*

That evening, Angelina made the after-supper coffee. *Will they notice how shiny the pot is now?*

No one said a word save Betty. "Yuck, what happened to the coffee!" she blurted.

"What's wrong with it?" Angelina asked.

"It tastes like bleach."

"Oh, no!" Angelina said.

"Did you bleach the coffee pot?"

"Well, yes. It was dirty, so I did."

"Don't you know you're never supposed to bleach an aluminium coffee pot?" Betty reproached her. "It makes the coffee taste awful."

Angelina's face dropped. "I'm sorry. I didn't know. I've never used an aluminium coffee pot before."

"Hey, it's okay," Anton consoled her. "Don't worry about it. It's just a coffee pot. The taste will go away."

"Yeah, don't worry, the taste will go away," Marie agreed.

18

MARIE WAS IN LABOUR. Angelina picked up the phone—Anton had had one installed a week earlier—and asked the switchboard operator to direct her call to the doctor's house.

His wife answered. "I'm sorry, but the doctor isn't in right now." There was a pause then she added, "He's tending to an emergency."

"Will you please tell him when he gets home that my sister, Marie Wiebe, is in labour?"

The woman promised she would.

"Is the doctor coming?" Marie asked.

"He's on an emergency call. But I'm sure he'll be here soon." At the look of dismay on Marie's face, Angelina added, "Don't worry, dear. There's plenty of time. Your pains are still far apart."

Two hours later, the doctor still hadn't phoned. So Angelina called once again.

"He's still not home," the doctor's wife said.

"Isn't there some way you can get a hold of him? My sister's contractions are getting stronger."

There was a sharp intake of breath on the other end. "Look, I'm going to be honest with you. There was no emergency case tonight. The truth is that my husband was out drinking. He's home now but he is passed out, drunk. I'll keep doing my best to wake him, but don't count on him coming."

"Is there another doctor somewhere I can phone?"

"Not nearby. I'm so sorry." There was regret and humiliation in her voice.

Oh no! Angelina hung up the phone.

"Anton, Anton!" Angelina shook him awake. "Anton," she whispered, "You're going to have to get up. I will need your help. Marie is in labour, but the doctor won't be coming."

Anton sat upright. "Won't be coming?" he asked alarmed.

"No, his wife said that he is passed out, drunk."

"But...what are we going to do?"

"I'll have to do it."

"But—but...can you?"

"I was there by Papa's side when he delivered my sister, Rosea. I was only seven at the time, but I remember it clear as day." Her Mama hadn't wanted her to be there, but there had been no one else around to help Papa—Rosea had come early and unexpectedly.

"And then another time, when I was twelve, I helped my Grosma Ginter deliver a neighbour's baby." Angelina paused then added, "We have no choice, Anton."

Angelina made another call. "Operator, I would like you to connect me to Janice Miller, my sister Betty lives with her."

By now the operator knew what was going on. She plugged in the circuit number. The phone began to ring.

After what seemed like ages, a sleepy voice answered. "Hello, Miller residence."

"This is Mrs. Jaslo calling. Pardon me for phoning at such an early hour but may I please talk with Betty. It's an emergency. Our sister is in labour and the doctor can't come out."

"Oh, oh, certainly," the girl said, now fully awake. "I'll go get her."

Angelina could hear Betty's roommate talking in the background. "Your sister is on the phone. Marie is having her baby."

Betty picked up the receiver.

"Betty, we need you. Sis is having her baby, but the doctor can't come."

"What! But he has to!"

"Well, he isn't. He's drunk. Come as quickly as you can, and Betty..."

"What?"

"Pray."

By now Mandy was awake and crying, and Anton was trying to puzzle out how to attach a diaper to a wriggling child.

"No doctor!" Marie said with alarm when Angelina told her the news.

"It'll be all right. Don't forget I've helped deliver babies before. Papa taught me. Papa delivered most of Mama's babies. Mama told me a couple of years ago that the births Papa helped her with went much easier than the ones in the hospital did."

Another wave of pain hit Marie. She grabbed Angelina's hand. "Don't leave me."

"I'll stay here right by your side, dear."

Less than an hour later, Betty walked in the door, her honey-blond hair soaked. "It's raining cats and dogs out there," she panted. "I ran most of the way." She rushed to Marie's side. "You okay, sis?"

With Betty there for Marie, Angelina was now able to direct her attention toward preparations for the birth.

"Anton," Angelina asked, "do you know where there is good strong rope?"

"I think I can find some," he answered.

"Good. I would like you to put a hook in the ceiling above the bed and tie the rope to it, good and tight. Let the other end of the rope dangle a few inches above the bed."

Anton handed the crying Mandy to Angelina and set about doing what she had requested. When he had finished, Angelina asked him to try and find something hollow, "like a pipe about a foot across."

He found an old bicycle handle and, following Angelina's instructions, looped the end of the rope through and tied it. Marie now had something to hang onto when active labour started.

Angelina sterilized a pair of scissors and set out towels. Then the waiting game began. Moans and cries of, "It hurts!" alternating with curses of "Damn that man!" grew closer together and increased in intensity.

Pre-dawn crept through the window, followed by morning light. Mandy had gone back to sleep, then woken again. Anton was doing his best to spoon cereal into the little tot's hungry mouth when Angelina asked Betty to bring the jar of lard she had made ready.

"It aids in the delivery, Papa said."

A few minutes later, baby Gregory announced his arrival with a loud wail.

While Betty cleaned him, Angelina kneaded Marie's abdomen to help her expel the afterbirth and slow down the bleeding.

Once the precious new life was ensconced in his mother's arms, Angelina grabbed Anton and Betty and danced in a little circle with them.

"Alleluia! Praise God!" they shouted.

19

"SIS," ANGELINA ASKED Marie during a solemn moment. "Does Bob ever hit you?"

Marie snorted. "He knows better. He knows that if he ever tried, I'd kill him."

"I heard what Papa did to you. I'm sorry."

"Yeah, well, it wasn't your fault."

"Why did he—?"

Marie cut her off. "I don't want to talk about it."

"But Marie, it's good to talk about it. It helps."

"She said she doesn't want to talk about it," Betty, visiting again, threw in. "Leave it be."

"I heard there's going to be a dance at the school this Saturday night," Anton interposed.

"Yeah, Janice and I and a couple of other friends are going to whoop it up," Betty said. "Are you going, Anton?"

"I'm not sure."

"Oh, come on, quit being a flat tire," Betty admonished her brother-in-law.

"Well, I know I sure would like to go," Angelina remarked.

After the war, Angelina and Joe had taken to frequenting the local legion hall; a house band played there every weekend. It hadn't taken long for the couple's dancing prowess to become known; the other patrons would applaud and move aside when they saw the duo step out onto the floor—the handsome, well-dressed gentleman, and his exquisite, beautiful lady with golden locks that fell to her waist.

How Angelina loved it. For a time she would be one in mind and spirit with Joe. For a time she would be his equal. And she would be loved and admired by everyone around her as well. She smiled now, thinking of it...

The band would start out with a laidback song like "The Tennessee Waltz," then switch midstride to a foxtrot:

You say e-ither and I say ei-ther,
you say ne-ither and I say nei-ther.
E-ither, ne-ither,
ei-ther, nei-ther,
let's call the whole thing off...

Hoping to catch the two dancers off guard, the orchestra then leaped mid-song into a sexy jive—the chorus of Glenn Miller's "In the Mood."

The frenzied audience would cheer as the dark, virile man effortlessly swung the pretty little blond down between his legs, up over his shoulder and back into his arms without losing a beat, the brass blaring in exuberance as they hit the high notes.

Then, as the band hit the verse, the couple's boldy flir-

tatious moves echoed the sultry woodwinds, slowing a bit; their hips taunted each other with mirrored desire. Tension and heat built between the skilled master and his lovely little innocent.

All eyes were on the handsome sheik and the softly curved maiden, gown twirling about her knees as she anticipated his every move.

Then once again they climaxed into full swing as the band played on. Putting everyone in the mood.

Then the band would switch gears again, slowing right back down to a waltz.

Joe and Angelina never faltered as everyone followed them down from the high point to which they had led them.

When they finally took a rest, people would clamour to join them and buy them drinks.

"Oh, how lucky you are to have a man like him," women would croon when Joe slipped away to the men's room. Everyone thought they were the ideal couple; no one suspected otherwise...

Angelina brought herself back to the present. "It would be nice to spiffy up for a change," she said to her sisters.

"I'm going too," Marie said. "I've been cooped up in this house long enough already."

THE THREE OF them walked to the school Saturday evening, with Anton holding Mandy, Angelina carrying Gregory, and Marie swinging a cloth sack filled with diapers and a couple of baby blankets.

"We're really going to whoop it up tonight!" Marie said excitedly.

Jake Penner and his band were warming up their instruments when the trio walked in. Angelina and Marie went to work settling the babies down on the floor in the back room alongside several others already there before joining Betty and the other girls and women sitting on the benches.

The band opened with an Art Mooney hit: "I'm Looking Over a Four-Leaf Clover."

Like most of the girls, Angelina sat through that tune and several others, waiting to be asked to dance, while the boys stood congregating in a corner.

Then the caller announced, "Okay, ladies' choice!"

Finally! Angelina went up to the group of men. Anton was standing with them. "Okay, Anton," she said. "Let's dance."

Anton put a hand on Angelina's waist as the lead guitarist opened a rendition of one of Les Brown's songs.

"Gonna take a sentimental journey," Penner began to sing.

Gonna set my heart at ease.
Gonna take a sentimental journey
to renew old memories.
Got my bag and got my reservation,
spent each dime I could afford.
Like a child in wild anticipation,
long to hear that 'All aboard!'

They didn't stir up an audience; Anton's moves weren't as smooth as Joe's—and there wasn't the striking contrast of fair maiden with her dark, dashing knight. No, Angelina and Anton could be better likened to a handsome matched pair of palomino ponies. But she felt right in his arms, as though she belonged in them.

The foxtrot ended and Angelina hoped for another dance with Anton but was whisked away instead by a short older gent, whose big bronco belt buckle called attention to his expansive belly. He sang along as they polkaed to Vaunghn Monroe's "Ghost Riders in the Sky."

"Yip-ee-ai-ay!" the stout man yowled in her ear, whirling her around.

Angelina next waltzed with a lanky farm boy who towered above her four-foot-eleven inches and held her as though she were made of fine china.

Dancer number four was a businessman, Tom, from Ottawa, visiting his brother. "I've been watching your moves," he commented. "You can dance. Where are you from?"

"I'm originally from around Saskatoon but now I live in Windsor," Angelina replied. "You can dance too. Have you ever been to the Casa Loma Ballroom?"

"I've been there a time or two. Too bad this town is so backwards. We could really swing together." Tom moved her a little faster.

He held onto her for the next dance as well, a much-slowed down version of Ella Fitzgerald's "Makin' Whoopee."

"You're a beautiful woman," Tom whispered to Angelina. "I hope you don't take offence at what I'm about to say...I'm a rich man. I could show you a very good time."

Angelina smiled.

"I'm flattered, Tom, and thank you for asking me. But no. I'm here for my sister and I'll soon be going back home to my husband."

"Your husband is a very lucky man. You are a real lady."

If he only knew.

Angelina noticed her sisters on the bench. After the ladies' choice dance they had sat back down. *Why do they come to a dance to just sit?*

Jake called out a square dance and after that another

polka, which Angelina danced to with Bronco Buckle. Before she could sit down, Penner announced a waltz.

"May I have this dance, ma'am?" she heard a voice say behind her. It was Anton.

"Most assuredly, sir," she answered, a bit coquettishly.

As Angelina moved in his arms, a feeling began to come over her. A feeling she had never before felt for a man—an aching, burning need to get closer.

Is this what Joe means when he says, "I'd just like to crawl up inside of you"?

Feeling unaccustomedly shy, Angelina avoided Anton's eyes. She was silent for the remainder of the waltz.

The band took a break and Angelina joined her sisters outside.

"I suppose you think you're the cat's meow now, don't you?" Betty hissed at her.

"No! Why would you say something like that?"

"Hoofin' it up with all the men. You've got a man at home, but that isn't good enough for you, is it? You want them all."

"That isn't true! I'm here to dance, not to find a man!"

"Yeah, I bet," Betty harrumphed. She and Marie moved away to join their circle of friends and take a sip from the bottle being passed around.

Anton sauntered over her way.

"It's a beautiful night, isn't it," Angelina commented.

"Yes, very beautiful," he answered, his hazel eyes looking straight into hers.

Angelina blushed, her breath caught in her throat.

At that moment the band started back up.

"Come on, let's dance," Angelina said hurriedly, uttering the first thing that popped into her head.

It was another waltz:

When a star is born,
they possess a gift or two,
one of them is this: they have the power to
make a wish come true.
When you wish upon a star,
makes no difference who you are,
anything your heart desires will come to you.
If your heart is in your dream,
no request is too extreme
when you wish upon a star as dreamers do.
Fate is kind; she brings to those who love
the sweet fulfillment of their secret longing.
Like a bolt out of the blue,
Fate steps in and sees you through
when you wish upon a star,
your dreams come true.

Do I dare to wish and long? Do dreams come true?

Angelina rested her head on Anton's shoulder and the couple danced through the night.

At the end of the social, a midnight lunch was served, after which the trio—Marie, Angelina and Anton—carrying the babies and diaper bag, began the trek home.

A myriad of stars blinked in approval as Anton slipped his hand through Angelina's.

20

ANGELINA SAT AT the kitchen table. Tears rolled down her cheeks.

"Why are you crying?" Betty, down for a couple of days, asked her.

"I was reading in the paper about a young man who died in a car accident," Angelina replied, dabbing her eyes.

"Who is he?"

"It says here his name is Samuel Rouse."

"You don't know him?"

"No."

"You mean you're bawling about someone you don't even know?"

"Well, I started thinking about how his poor family must be suffering and..."

"What a dumb Dora, you're strangers!"

"That doesn't matter."

Betty stared at her sister in silence for a moment, then

said, "You know, sometimes I wonder if you don't just put on an act."

"An act? No...why would I want to do that?" Angelina was incredulous. "Don't you remember how Mama prayed every Saturday night for all the drunks out there—that they'd get home safely?"

Betty ignored her reply. "So, when are you going back home?" she asked. "Now that Bob is back, Marie doesn't really need you here anymore."

"I've decided I'm not going back."

"What! Does Joe know that?"

"I wrote him a couple of weeks ago and told him. I also told him that I had found someone else." Angelina paused. "Anton and I are in love. When I'm with him, I feel alive and happy. We're going to get our own house and move in together."

"Hey, look, we all know the two of you have been making whoopee, but you can't stay with him."

"Why not?"

"Well..." her sister stuttered, "for one thing, you're married!"

"Anton has offered to help me pay for a divorce."

"You're just using him."

"No, I'm not! We love each other and we want to get married."

It was true. She had finally found true love. She and Anton had realized their feelings for each other the night of the dance and had made sweet love afterwards. He was so gentle, so patient with her. Something Joe had never been.

How wonderful, too, it felt to be with a man of her own people; a man with similar traditions, a man who spoke the language of her childhood. Joe forbade her to speak any words of *Plautdietsch* when he was around. He said that he had been told it wasn't real Dutch—or even German, for that matter—that it was a type of pig Latin.

"And I'm pregnant," Angelina continued.

"You're *what!*"

"Yes. Anton and I planned it. It's our love child."

"But you can't do this. You just can't!"

"Why not? I know you think Joe's such a nice man. You don't know what he's really like. He always puts on a big show around all of you."

"I don't believe that. I think it's *you.* And if he does hit you, you probably do something to deserve it, like...like you're doing now." Betty spun around and walked out the door.

THE NEXT DAY the phone rang and Betty raced to pick up the receiver. "Hello, just a minute," she said. "It's for you, Angelina," she called.

Maybe it's Anton, Angelina thought. To her shock and dismay, it was Joe.

"How did you get this number?" she asked.

"Betty was kind enough to give it to me." There was a pause. "When are you coming home?"

"Didn't you get my letter?"

"Yes. I received it. You know, they don't want you there."

"That's a lie."

"Is it? Ask them."

She let that drop and said, "I told you in the letter. I have a new man and I want a divorce."

"Do you really, now?" His tone was mocking. "You know that no man could ever know you as well as I do—your every thought, your every move."

It was on her tongue to say that that wasn't true. That he didn't know her at all. But she couldn't, for in truth he had often read her mind. She remembered one night when he had pinned her down in bed after beating her. He had looked deep into her eyes and said, in a low, taunting voice, "I know what you're thinking. You're wishing I were in a locked cage so that you could torture me, aren't you?" His words had been close, very close to the truth.

"Tell me," he now said, "when the two of you dance, are you one, as you and I are?"

"That's beside the point. Anton and I love each other—and I'm going to have his baby."

"I'll tell you this, no man on earth can ever love you as much as I do. I'll prove it. I'm willing to take you back, baby and all. Come back to me, and I swear I will love it and treat it as my own."

"Joe, I told you. I've found someone new."

He changed tactics. "You say he loves you. Well, I challenge you to try him out. Tell him you've decided to come back to me and see what he says. See if he'll try to stop you."

"Okay. I will!"

"All right, my love. I'll say good night for now but I'll phone again tomorrow." He paused. "I love you."

Angelina hung up the phone.

"Why," she asked Betty, "did you give him our number?"

"He had a right to know," Betty retorted. "So are you going back to him?"

"No, I am not!" Angelina insisted. "I want to be with Anton!"

"Just like you wanted so badly to be with Joe?" Betty said. "I saw you all those years ago—the two of you smooching and carrying on. You sure didn't seem to mind him then."

"That was before I found out just what kind of man he is," Angelina argued.

"Well, like I said, I think you ask for it. I think you like to be hit. In the barn when Dad was going to give you a lickin', you'd get down on your knees and try to kiss his hands, remember? He'd be hitting you and you'd be hollerin', 'I love you, Papa. I love you!' It made me sick. You reminded me of a dog licking his master's hands. *I* sure didn't do that when Papa hit me."

"It was because I knew it wasn't really me he was hitting—in his heart it was Mama."

"You and your stupid ideas! When he was hitting you, or me, or any one of us, it was *us* he was beating, not Mom. Us! *Us!*" Betty screamed.

She grabbed the broom. "I'm sick of you and your ideas and you thinking you're better than us. Go home where you belong!"

"No!"

Betty began hitting Angelina with the broom. "I said, 'Go home!' We don't want you here!"

Marie, watching, said nothing.

Angelina fled to the bedroom in tears. *It's true! My sisters don't love me! They don't want me!*

When Anton came home that night he could see she had been crying. "What's wrong?" he asked.

"Oh, oh, nothing," she answered. The question was on her lips but she couldn't ask it; she didn't feel strong enough.

But she had to know and so the next day she walked to town and went to see him at his shop. "Joe got a hold of our number and begged me yesterday to return to him. Betty and Marie think I should."

"And are you?" Anton asked.

"With everyone telling me to, it looks like I don't have much choice. I might have to go back to him whether I want to or not." Angelina searched his face desperately.

Anton turned his attention back to the shoe he was repairing with a sigh. "Well, I guess you have to do what you have to do."

My mother returned to Joe.

Years later, Mom wrote her own version of Kitty's Well's "There Must be Another Way to Live":

Oh, there must be another way to live.
Oh, yes, there must be another way to live.
I shook and trembled as the blood ran down my face;
I looked around to find a hiding place
but all I could think of was,
Lord, there must be another way to live.

Oh, there must be another way to live
and people will say, 'Forget it ever happened,'
and it's so easy for them to say it never happened.
But I can surely say it feels like yesterday
as he left the room,
I felt full of gloom,
'cause I looked up and I could see
the blood trickling down the wall
and knew, oh Lord, it was from me!

I fell down on my knees and cried out to God,
'Lord, please, oh Lord, have mercy on me
for surely, oh surely, there must be another way to live.'
It happened in 1949 and I wish
I could get it out of my mind.
There must be another way to live.

Part Two
1954 - 1965

21

SOMETHING WAKES ME up. A sound. I listen.

There...again.

What is that noise?

A small figure topped with a halo of moon-coloured hair, I creep out of bed. I open the bedroom door and peer into the living room.

Mommy is on the couch. Daddy is beside her.

I edge closer.

Daddy's got his hands on Mommy's throat. Mommy is making funny noises. *Mommy can't breathe!*

"Daddy! Daddy! You're hurting Mommy!"

HOW I LOVED my father. I loved my mommy too, but Daddy was the one who took me to places like the one that had pony rides and all those pretty lights in the sky. When I had been scared to go on that bridge with no end—the one that sometimes breaks in the middle—he stopped the car and hugged me and told me it didn't really break. It just looked like that. People made it open sometimes to let big boats go underneath. He said he would never let them open it when we were on it.

One night there was loud thunder and I was scared, but Daddy put me on his knee and said that that was just lightning's voice. It couldn't hurt me. And Daddy sometimes helped me pick pretty rocks at the waterfalls that went all the way up to the moon. And one time he even went all the way to the North Pole, driving through blizzards, just to get me Snowball, my Eskimo dog. Daddy always called me his special little angel, his good little girl.

Every evening, I would wait anxiously for the sound of his car in the driveway. "Daddy, Daddy!" I would cry excitedly as he walked through the door.

Whenever I heard the words to "How Far is Heaven," I would break into tears:

A little girl was waiting for her daddy one day.
It was time to meet him when she heard
her mommy say,
'Come to Mommy, darling, please do not cry,
Daddy's gone to heaven, way up in the sky.'

How far is heaven?
When can I go
to see my daddy? He's there, I know.
How far is heaven?
Let's go tonight.
I want my daddy to hold me tight.

"Zat poor little girl has no daddy no more," I'd sob. "He'z dead and gone to heaven."

Yes, I loved my daddy and I knew he loved me too.

BUT NOW I rushed forward to Mommy's defence.

"Daddy! Stop! You're hurting Mommy."

He let go of Mommy. With the back of his hand, he sent me flying into the side of the wall.

"You little brat!" he bellowed, "I'm not your real father. And I don't love you. I never have!"

Too shocked to cry, I pulled myself off the floor and made my way to the opposite side of the room. Seating myself in my little rocking chair, I began to rock.

My daddy says he don't love me no more. He says he don't never love me. It's all been just pretend like them people on shows. He just pretended he loved me. He says he isn't even my daddy! Well, I don't love him no more, neither. I hate him! I hate him!

I didn't hear his approaching footsteps.

"I'm so sorry, Korel. I didn't mean it. Daddy's so sorry."

I don't hear you.

I didn't see the tears pouring down his face. I didn't see the trembling hand he reached out to me, his heretofore adoring little girl.

I rocked faster.

I don't see you.

He's not my daddy. He's Joe. His name is Joe.

22

EARLY MORNING SUNLIGHT streamed through the window, spinning my mother's long waves into pure gold.

Joe stood admiring her from the doorway, a tray in his hands. "Angelina, I've made you breakfast."

He set down the offering on the night table.

Mom opened her tearstained eyes, and sat up in bed. Her lovely face was pale and her throat sported large bruises.

"Oh, my angel, you don't know how beautiful you look when you've been crying. Right now you're the most beautiful woman in the world. I love you so much!" He brushed a fingertip against her swollen lips.

She recoiled.

"Please don't pull away from me, darling. I know you're frightened. I'm sorry. I realize I lost control last night. It's just that you make me so angry sometimes. You've got to stop doing that, sweetheart. I don't like to get angry with you. Here, honey, take a bite of egg. I made it just the way you like it."

My mother held her tongue, afraid to rock the boat, afraid for me, Korel, her three-year old daughter, still sleeping. She knew that I adored Joe and that the love was mutual. In his eyes, I could do no wrong. I was his good little girl.

Mom thought back to the night before. She had tried so hard, as she had countless other times, to hide Joe's violent side from me.

This time it had been over a jar of preserves.

Joe had been saying for weeks that he missed his mother's beet relish. But they had moved to the small town of Coaldale, Alberta, where Angelina's sister Kathy and her husband lived, a few months ago and Ontario was now far away. So yesterday morning, she had phoned her mother-in-law out in New Toronto and got the recipe. She then spent the rest of the day preparing and canning the relish.

Joe had come home from work in a foul mood. The boss at the brewery where he worked in the nearby city of Lethbridge had sent him down the ladder to clean the interior of the vats again. Each time he cleaned them, he felt sick for days afterwards from the overwhelming ammonia fumes.

"I'm always the one he picks," he complained, "It's never Preston or that Nazi, Duerkson. *I'm* always the one. 'Let the Polack, Jaslo, do it.' That's what they think."

Later in the evening, after they had settled me for the night, Joe opened a jar of the relish and tasted it.

"You call this relish?" he had bellowed, "Are you incapable of doing *anything* right?" He threw the jar, narrowly missing her.

"I'm sorry, Joe. I'm sorry. Please. Shhh, you're going to wake up Korel."

"And I'm tired of you telling me to be quiet all the time!" Fist raised, he advanced towards her.

Backing away, she fell onto the sofa.

"*I* am boss of this house. Do you hear me?" he bent her head back over the arm of the couch and began choking her.

At that point she passed out.

When she came to, she saw me sitting in a corner of the living room in my little rocker, with Joe kneeling beside me, begging for forgiveness. She stumbled towards me.

I didn't look up. I wasn't crying. I was just quietly sitting there, rocking. Then she saw me suddenly rise and, zombie-like, head back to bed.

HAD THEIR ARGUMENT wakened me, my mother now worried. Had I witnessed the entire thing? Was that why Joe had been apologizing to me?

23

IT WAS MORNING. I could hear the soft murmur of my parents' voices. I lie awake, thinking.

Daddy don't sound mad no more and Mommy isn't crying. I know! Mommy and Daddy were just doing pretend. That's it! Daddy wasn't really hurting Mommy. He was just pretending to, like on a show. But why do Mommy and Daddy want to pretend that? I know! They were making a play for me to see. That's it! And Daddy really is my daddy and he really does *love me.*

After Daddy left for work, Mommy came into my room. She still wore the "pretend" bruises on her neck.

"I'm so sorry, Korel," she cried.

Why is Mommy crying? Why is Mommy saying sorry? Is she scared I think it's for real?

I wrapped my arms around her and smiled. "It's okay, Mommy. I know you and Daddy were just doing pretend. I know Daddy didn't really hurt you. And he didn't mean what he said to me neither. I know it was all just pretend, a play you and Daddy made for me."

"What did Daddy say to you?"

"He said that he wasn't my real daddy. He said that he didn't love me no more."

Mommy cried harder and hugged me. "You're right, sweetie. Mommy and Daddy were just pretending to fight. He didn't mean anything he said. Oh, Korel. I love you so much."

"I love you too, Mommy."

A COUPLE OF weeks later my parents put on another "show" for me. *I don't like that play. It isn't funny. Mommy's pretend blood scares me.* I covered my ears and retreated to the quiet of my closet.

24

WEEKS SHY OF my fourth birthday, I lay in a hospital bed. I was receiving a blood transfusion.

"Your daughter is very sick," Dr. McPherson, the child specialist, informed my parents, "I suspect it's rheumatic fever. To complicate matters, she is also anemic and suffering from severe malnutrition. Her heart is faltering and likely inflamed. We've got to try to get her fever down. I think it only right that I warn you—she may not make it through the night."

"Oh, God, no!" my mother gasped. She stood beside my hospital bed, wracked with guilt. "Why, oh why didn't I listen to myself?" she castigated.

Months earlier she had sensed something was wrong—I had stopped eating...

"MOMMY, I DON'T like food," I began complaining one day. "Food tastes like cow poop smells."

"But Korel, you've got to eat."

"But why, Mommy? I just poop it out again."

And with each passing day I ate less.

"Please, Korel, just a few bites. For Mommy?" she coaxed.

I would open my mouth, accept a small spoonful, swallow and nearly gag. Big, silent tears would roll down my cheeks. Joe tried tempting me with ice cream and cake, but I protested, saying that they tasted even worse.

"Well," Joe said," if food really does taste as foul to Korel as her breath smells, I can understand her disgust."

She brought me to the family physician, Dr. Robinson. He told her that my tonsils were inflamed and wrote out a prescription. "I wouldn't be too concerned about her appetite, though," he added. "She's just going through a phase. Many children her age do. When she gets hungry enough, she'll eat."

I didn't.

My health began to deteriorate—I started coming down with one cold after another.

My mother had other concerns about me as well. She was beginning to notice a change in my personality.

I had always been such a bright, inquisitive little girl. It was always, "why this," or "why that?" Like the first time I went on a train:

The porter, a Negro, had passed by our seat, and I had asked in a loud voice, "Mommy, why is that man so dirty?" I had never seen a black man before.

Mortified, but thinking quickly, she had answered, "He isn't dirty, dear, it's like this. When God first made people, they were all white. You know, like a colouring book is?"

I had nodded.

"Then God started to colour them. He coloured some people brown, some people black, some yellow and red. But

then he suddenly ran out of paint and so some of us had to stay white."

The man, hearing this, had broken into laughter. "Missus," he said, "I've heard a lot of stories in my day, but that one beats them all. Yep, he done ran out of paint...."

But lately the questions had all but stopped, and I had become dull and listless. I frequently sought out reassurance of her love for me and demanded more and more of her attention. One day, when she had been busy canning, I had said to her, "I know somesing. My Mommy don't love me no more."

I had also taken to sleeping in my closet. She would tuck me into bed at night and then find me in my closet in the morning, my bed neatly made.

"Why don't you want to sleep in your bed, Korel?" she had asked me once.

"I don't like messing it up," I had answered.

That would seem to make sense, she had reasoned.

When I was two, Joe had bought me the bed. Its frame was made of pine with a blond finish and on its headboard, Joe had engraved the words "Korel's Bed." For me it had been love at first sight and I took care of it well. I faithfully put together my night covers each morning, carefully smoothing out the bedspread. Then I arranged several of my dolls and stuffed animals by the pillows. A few times a week, I took a damp cloth and wiped the frame, being careful not to dislodge the Disney character decals of Mickey Mouse, Cinderella and Snow White that Joe and I had pasted on the headboard. The bed was the only piece of furniture Mommy and Joe had had shipped when they had moved to Alberta. Joe had been unable to stand the tears he had seen streaming down my cheeks when he had told me we would have to leave it behind.

Yes, my mother understood that I liked to keep my things neat and tidy, but...

25

THE RHEUMATIC FEVER had been caused by strep throat left untreated. How long after the streptococci bacteria had invaded my body had the fever set in? Two to three weeks. My mother thought back to what had been going on at that time.

There was the morning she had decided to give the kitchen a thorough cleaning...

As soon as Joe had left for work, she had begun emptying the cupboards, taking down the curtains.

Before long, she had boxes of food sitting on the living room floor, and the red and white checkered curtains soaking in the tub. She was in the midst of piling dishes, plates, bowls and cups on the sofa and chairs when I crawled out of bed.

"Mommy, my throat hurts," I whined.

I had had that sore throat for over a week by then. She

had brought me once again to the doctor. He had diagnosed it as the flu.

"Another cold!" My mother had protested. "I think it's because of those tonsils. I wish you would just take them out once and for all. She's not eating and she keeps getting sick."

"I'd rather wait until she's a little older to remove her tonsils," the doctor had said. "In regards to her appetite, you'd be surprised at how little food children her age really need, especially girls. And she is particularly petite."

I don't remember my sisters eating so little, *she had thought.*

She now touched my forehead with the inside of her wrist. I was still running a bit of a fever. She doctored me up with yet another aspirin, Vicks on the neck and chest and in the nose, and a hot toddy made of milk, cloves, honey and butter. She struggled to get me to eat a few mouthfuls of oatmeal, but I refused. At least she's getting some nutrition from the toddy.

"Mommy, I want to lay down but there's stuff on the couch," I grumbled.

"Well, Mommy is trying to clean the kitchen today. How about you lie down in my bed?" She knew that was always a treat for me.

She began washing the walls. Once done, she went to check on me. I was asleep. She stood by the bed and gently smoothed down my hair, which stuck out in all directions like an albino hedgehog.

"I don't think you know how precious you are to me," she softly whispered. "The doctor wasn't sure you would be born because I kept bleeding while I was carrying you and there was the radiation from all those X-rays they had to keep giving me too. But you were a fighter and you hung in

there. You were born without eyebrows or eyelashes—you didn't get any hair until you were two—and you had no toenails or fingernails, but you made it! And to me you were the prettiest baby alive. I thank God every day for you."

She went back to work preparing flour glue, as she wanted to paper one of the walls. She had chosen a pattern with red carnations—red was her favourite colour and carnations her favourite flower. Once the wallpaper was up, she wiped the inside of the drawers. Hmm. They could use new liners. I know what I'll do, I'll use some of the leftover wallpaper. *By now it was approaching noon and I was up again. She coaxed me into eating a couple of mouthfuls of creamed corn, one of the few foods I had any degree of amicable feeling for.*

"Mommy, could you read me a story?" I asked.

"Oh, honey, I'm sorry but I don't have time today. I've got to get all this done before Daddy gets home." She thought for a moment. "Tell you what. I'm going to cut out liners for the drawers. How about you take the paintbrush and smear this glue on the paper for me and we'll sing while we're working."

I began gluing. "Mommy, you sing. It hurts my s'roat when I sing. Sing me again that song about that girl who has no Mommy."

After a few seconds of figuring out which song I meant she began to sing:

I once had a dear, kind Mommy,
who was always good to me
and in my times of trouble
she would sit me on her knee,

but one night as I lay sleeping
in my trundle bed
an angel sat down beside me
and told me my Mommy was dead.

When I awoke the next morning,
I found that it was true:
my mommy had gone to heaven
in the sky so blue.

So children be good to your Mommies,
I mean both big and small,
for when you have no Mommy,
you have nothing at all.
Yes, when you have no Mommy,
you have nothing at all.

The tears streamed down my face. "Please, Mommy," I said. "Don't you never die and leave me."

She put down the scissors and hugged me. "Oh, sweetheart, I'll never leave you! I love you so much."

I glued for a while, then said I was tired and went back to bed.

My mother watched me go. She's so skinny and she eats so little. I just know that's why she keeps getting sick. Why won't the doctor listen to me?

The hours went by. She glanced at the clock. Joe was going to be home soon and the kitchen and living room were still in a state of disarray.

He's going to be mad. But I don't give a damn. I'm sick and tired of thinking about what His Royal Highness does and doesn't like.

Joe came home and asked for his supper. She brought

him a plate of roast pork, fried potatoes and corn left over from the previous dinner.

"You give me this!" he roared, "I work hard all day, and this—" he dumped the food on the floor—"is my thank you?"

"I've been so busy today trying to get this kitchen done..."

"You just sit and let this place become a pigsty and then all of a sudden you get this idea in your head that you're going to clean it, one room at a time. And who has to suffer? I do."

"I try to make you happy, but all you ever do is pick on me. I'm tired of it," she stated, sweeping up the remains of his meal.

"Don't talk back to me, woman," he snarled, shoving her against the edge of the cupboard. He grabbed her by the bodice of her dress. His eyes, now manic black, bored into hers. "We'll just see who's the boss around here."

Oh God, no! I've pushed him too far. *"No, no. I'm sorry, Joe. I'm sorry."*

He dragged her into the bedroom.

She couldn't stifle her cry of pain.

Early the next morning she lost the three-month old fetus she had been carrying. She began to hemorrhage.

Joe, afraid for her life, brought her to the hospital.

26

WITH HIS WIFE in the hospital, Joe now had the problem of finding someone to look after his daughter. He could have asked his sister-in-law, Kathy, who lived nearby, but they weren't too fond of each other.

One day, he had seen Angelina and Kathy sitting at the table, snacking. Sitting there, whittling away time, talking and nibbling, when there had been dishes waiting to be washed!

"Why are you snacking?" he had inquired. "You just had a big meal."

His sister-in-law had glared at him. "You don't like me *shmangin'?*" She had deliberately taunted him by using that word instead of the one in English because she knew he didn't like that inferior language, that pig Latin, being spoken in his house. "Well, just watch this!"

To his horror, she had begun grabbing and stuffing food into her mouth, so much so that it had formed a pouch like a hamster's and bits of half-chewed morsels had plopped onto the table. In disgust, he had left the room. That woman had absolutely no respect for a man.

No, he would not ask Kathy for her help. He decided to ask his cousin Judy instead. She and her husband had children of their own and had recently moved from Ontario to Lethbridge.

Judy agreed to take me in until my mother came home but she was less than thrilled with the idea. *Miss Prissy*, she thought, that's what I was. Everything I wore had to match. If I had on a blue dress, I would insist that my socks and hair ribbon and even my panties be blue as well. *What a spoiled brat!* And she remembered the day, about a year earlier, when both our families still lived in Ontario, that she and her three kids had come to visit. She had shooed her two youngest to "go play" and they did, in my bedroom. They had been playing for perhaps a half-hour when her four-year old, Sharon, suddenly came running into the living room. "Mommy! Mommy!" she had screamed. "Korel bit me!" And certainly her arm sported the imprint of my sharp little teeth.

Judy had been mortified, especially so when my mother, instead of immediately spanking me—as Judy had thought she should—had instead asked me, "Why did you bite Sharon, Korel?"

"Them kids keep bweaking my s'ings all'a time and S'awon scwibbled all over my bed," I had answered.

"Show me, Korel," my mother had said.

Judy had followed my mother into my room.

Sobbing, I had shown them the vivid red and green crayon markings on my bed's headboard and had then pointed to the floor where lay an ornament—a white dog, its right leg now severed.

Judy had given Sharon a spanking right on the spot

and felt that I deserved one as well. But I had been given only a talking to—had been told that should anything like that happen again I should not bite but immediately tell my mother. Judy couldn't believe it. I had gotten away with biting her child. And what normal kid bites someone over a bed or an ornament anyway? A toy, maybe, but a bed? Cripes, I had even drawn blood!

Well, if she was going to be looking after me, she now told Joe, I would be following her rules.

"SHE WON'T EAT, she cries over everything," Judy complained to Joe after the second day. "She's afraid of getting dirty. I've never seen a three year old—well, actually, she'll be four in a month—who's concerned about getting dirty before! She refuses to play with the kids. She just sits there."

"She hasn't been feeling well lately," he said stiffly, holding back an angry retort. Still, seeing no other option but to continue leaving me with her, he left.

27

THE DAYS WERE long and lonely as I waited for Joe's daily visits. I took to standing by the window and waiting for him.

I don't like it here! Auntie Judy is a real witch who lives in a big scary house. A monster lives here too. Cousin Billy told me so. He says that if I don't quit crying, the monster will eat me. I'm scared. He says it lives upstairs and it has a long neck and that it comes downstairs sometimes. One time I felt it grab my sweater. It did! Sometimes the monster hides under the bathtub too. But Billy says it's invisible then—he showed me. He put water in the bathtub then pulled out the plug. He put my hand over the hole and I felt the monster. It almost sucked me through the hole!

Auntie Judy doesn't like me. She says I'm a spoiled brat and she makes me wear ugly pants and clothes that don't match. I cried because I miss my Mommy and Daddy, and she got mad and she spanked me. Auntie Judy makes me eat and I throw up and she gets real mad.

I feel sick too. I'm cold and my legs hurt. I miss my room and my closet. I miss my Mommy too and my stomach feels funny. It feels like it's crying and it misses Mommy too. I don't like it when my stomach feels like that—it makes me throw up. I wish Mommy would come home, but she's sick too. I like it when Daddy comes to visit me. I wish he would take me home.

Each time Joe got ready to leave I would wrap my skinny little arms around him and beg him to stay.

On the third evening, I groused to him about sore legs. I had a fever and was developing a rash. Judy told Joe that she had phoned the doctor and he had told her it sounded like measles and that it was going around. "Just make sure she gets plenty of rest and fluids, and give her aspirin."

Joe decided to take a couple of days off from work to look after me himself.

He did as the doctor prescribed. Joe also gave me warm baths to try and ease the soreness in my legs. He set to work making homemade chicken noodle soup—the way he had seen his mother make it—and tried to get me to swallow some. "Your *bopcha* always gave me this when I was sick," he said.

I finally told him about the monster. I had been too scared to tell him about it at Auntie Judy's house. Even now I shivered.

He was confused at first and then it dawned on him. "Oh," he said, "I think you're talking about something called a vacuum cleaner."

I had never seen one before—we didn't own one.

"It's not a monster, it's a machine," he explained. "Billy was just trying to frighten you. A vacuum cleaner whirls air around inside it to suck up small things, like dirt, so you can clean the floor. It's like a straw that pulls up water when you suck on it. But don't be afraid—a vacuum cleaner isn't nearly big enough or strong enough to pick you up."

I felt less afraid of the "monster" after that but still avoided bathtub drains. To this day, the sight of swirling water makes me a little uncomfortable.

MY MOTHER WAS in the hospital for eight days. When Joe brought her home she was despondent. She noticed my rash and that I was sick in bed—again—but she took Joe's word for it that I had the measles. Somewhere in the back of her mind it must have registered that measles didn't look splotchy like a windburn, but she was tired, so very tired. She just wanted to sleep and sleep. She hugged me and spoke to me for a few minutes, then went to bed.

The following morning Joe returned to work and my mother, though she would have preferred to remain in bed, forced herself to get up so she could care for me.

When she came into my room, I was curled up like a ball and shivering.

"I'm c-c-cold, Mommy," I said through chattering teeth.

"Mommy will warm you up," she said. She sat beside me on my bed and opened the sash of her woolly red housecoat, then reached to wrap me inside it.

"Ow," I moaned, as she grabbed my arm.

Puzzled, she pulled up the sleeve of my pyjamas and saw, to her horror, a grossly swollen elbow. With urgency she pulled my nightshirt over my head, and discovered matching inflammation in the other elbow and in my shoulders. She pulled my pyjama bottoms down and gasped as she saw the stiff, distended limbs of my emaciated, splotchy-skinned child's body. The heat of the fever radiated out, and my muscles jerked sporadically.

"Oh, my God," she whispered. She called the ambulance.

When she tried to get me to stand to dress me, my legs buckled beneath me. She bundled me into a blanket and prayed for the ambulance to hurry.

I heard them talking. I heard them say I was very, very sick. But I thought that strange, since I didn't feel sick anymore. In fact, I felt better than I had for a long time. My throat didn't hurt, my head wasn't sore, my arms and legs didn't ache. I wasn't itchy, or cold, or shivery anymore. I tried telling them, but my mouth wouldn't work.

I'm not sick no more. I feel so nice and cozy, just like when I go into Mommy and Daddy's bed in the morning.

Something caught the corner of my eye. I turned my head. Christmas lights outside my window. More beautiful even than the ones Daddy had put on our Christmas tree. Green ones, greener than the lawn when the sky gets all dark and wet; red ones, redder than a stop light; and white ones, sparkly white, like snow when the moon shines on it.

Pretty, so pretty, so shiny. I looked and looked.

I heard singing and there at my feet fairies danced, their tiny feet moving to the music.

I wished my mouth worked so I could sing with them. I wanted to point them out to my mommy and daddy, but my hand didn't want to work either.

One of the fairies had a voice like Mommy's and hair like Mommy's. Another one wore a real pretty dress, the colour of a blue Easter egg. I stared and stared. *I like their happy song.*

I began to feel heavier and heavier, yet my head was light, a feather. I was hard rock but soft marshmallow too. I started whirling round and round like on a merry-go-round, a very fast merry-go-round. I was going so fast that I couldn't see Mommy and Daddy anymore. I couldn't see the doctor or the nurse, not even the room. I saw my dog Snowball chewing on a bone. I saw a waterfall that reached the moon. I saw myself riding on Daddy's shoulders as he walked down the cellar steps to get a jar of pickles. I saw stars—everywhere bright, shiny stars.

I went faster and faster.

This is fun!

The merry-go-round stopped suddenly and I was in a white place. It wasn't the hospital. It wasn't my house. It wasn't anyone's house. It didn't have a floor or a ceiling, but it wasn't outside either—it didn't have trees or grass or even a sky. Everything was white, like when it's foggy in the mountains—but it was a nice warm, cozy fog.

Then I saw the pretty lady. She was smiling.

"Life is just a dream, Korel. When you die, you wake up," she said.

"HOW COULD I have been so stupid not to realize just how sick my own daughter was?" my mother admonished herself. "Why didn't I force the doctor to do something? I'm a no-good mother!"

Joe took her hand. "Don't say that, Angelina. This isn't your fault. You're a very good mother. Korel couldn't ask for a better one." In spite of his often scathing words on other subjects, he never found fault with her mothering of me. "If anyone is to blame, it's me. I should have taken her to the doctor when I brought her home from Judy's."

They knelt at my bedside and prayed, begging for God's mercy. "You've already taken six children from us. Please, God, don't take our Korel yet too."

"If I lose her, I don't want to live anymore," Mom cried.

28

"We're getting her back," the nurse announced.

"Oh, thank God!" Mom and Joe cried in unison. They had been by my side all night.

I had been given an injection of penicillin, and vitamin B, a blood transfusion, and was hooked up to an intravenous bag. Because the veins in my arms and hands were fragile, the doctor had incised the large vein on the inside of my right thigh near the groin and inserted a shunt. My fever had been brought down with ice packs.

Doctor McPherson, the pediatrician, had a round face that was, in other circumstances, jocular and friendly, but was now red and sober. His eyes were frosty. He took my parents aside.

"That little girl was *very* close to dying," he said. "She's suffering not only from rheumatic fever, which is bad enough in itself, but from severe malnutrition and anemia as well. She's what? Almost four? And she weighs only twenty pounds. Why is that?"

My mother explained what the other doctor had said, adding, "...and then I was in the hospital for a week and Korel stayed with a sitter."

Dr. McPherson shook his head. "I know I'm not supposed to condemn another doctor's methods of practice, but Gregory is an exception to the rule. How he managed to receive his doctorate is beyond me. I wouldn't bring my cat to him."

He resumed his scolding. "Still, you should have followed your own head. A mother is usually a pretty good judge of whether or not something is wrong with her child." His face began to soften at my mother's stricken expression. "We've got her stable for now, but her immune system is very weak and we don't yet know the extent of damage to her heart."

For the first week Mom never left my room. She slept on a cot the staff provided and ate what was brought in to her on a tray. She took over much of my care. She checked my pulse frequently, and kept an eye on my temperature and my I.V. bag. She gave me daily sponge baths; I couldn't get out of bed, I was too weak and was hooked up to a catheter as well as the I.V.

But I begged for a soak in the tub. I had discovered before coming into the hospital that hot water drove away the dull ache and cold from my body—at least temporarily. When I slipped into its steamy embrace, I felt it going to work almost immediately. I would shiver as the heat drove the veil of cold down from my skin into muscle, and then further, from muscle into bone, and finally, from bone into oblivion.

Mom told me that if I ate a little, at least a spoonful or two, at every meal, I would grow strong enough to sit on a bedpan and the catheter could come out. Gagging on every mouthful, I did as she suggested. But when a nurse tried tempting me with a fudgesicle, I refused to taste it.

"It looks like poop on a stick," I protested to Mom once the kindly woman was out of earshot.

They wanted me to drink milk. I refused. "It goes down my throat all slimy, like snot," I grouched.

My mother requested dry skim milk powder. "She likes to eat it raw," she told the nurse.

"That's fine," Dr. McPherson accommodated, "if that's the way she likes it. It certainly won't hurt her any." He reconfirmed that I had tonsillitis. "That's likely what caused her initial disinterest in food. The vitamin B_{12} injections should increase her appetite."

Two weeks after I had been admitted, Dr. McPherson told my mother I was no longer on the critical condition list. Though tests revealed there were a number of leaky valves in my heart, there was a good chance I would recover. But, he added, I would probably need to stay in the hospital for another month and would need regular shots of penicillin for five years to ward off a reoccurrence of the rheumatic fever. When I was strong enough, and of sufficient weight, my tonsils would be removed.

The doctor suggested my mother could start spending nights at home.

She certainly did have things that needed taking care of at home, she agreed, but...what if something happened? What if her daughter took a turn for the worse?

They would notify her, he said, if any new complications arose.

"Honey," she said to me. "Mommy is going to go home tonight."

"But why? Why can't you stay here?"

"I have things to do at home. And well...Mommy does live there, you know."

"I live there too."

"Yes, it's your home too, but you have to stay here until you get better."

"I don't want to live here by myself," I protested.

"You *aren't* by yourself," she reassured me. "You've got all these nice nurses and Dr. McPherson."

Tears sprang to my eyes. "But they aren't *you.* I don't want you to go! Mommy, please don't go!" I pleaded.

"Look, Daddy is all alone. You don't want Daddy to be lonely, do you?"

"No."

"It's just for a day. I'll come back the day after tomorrow and visit with you all day, I promise. Now, I want you to be a good girl for the nurses, okay?"

"Okay," I sniffed.

"You promise?"

"Yes."

She left.

The spirit of abject aloneness that had bestowed itself upon me at Judy's house returned, wrapping itself in waves around my lower torso—a tight band around my abdomen and the small of my back. I felt nauseated and threw up the meagre contents of my stomach. Silent tears rolled down my hollow cheeks.

"Mommy," I whispered, "please come back."

MY MOTHER PHONED the next morning, and then again in the afternoon.

"She's fine," she was told.

At two a.m. she received the call. "Korel has taken a turn for the worse."

My mother and Joe raced the six miles back to the hospital.

I lay in bed with wires poking every which way out of my body. A new shunt had been placed in a vein on the opposite side of my groin, and I was receiving yet another blood transfusion. My heart was failing and my temperature had skyrocketed.

"Make her fight, Mother," Dr. McPherson said when my Mom walked into the room. "She doesn't want to live."

"Mommy's here, sweetheart. Everything will be all right. I'm here now."

I heard my mother's voice as if from a distance. She smoothed my sweat-drenched hair. "Korel, listen to me. You've got to get better. Please, for Mommy and Daddy!"

But I like being really sick. It feels nice. I'm warm. I don't want that bad dream no more.

"Mommy and Daddy need you."

I didn't want to open my eyes. I didn't want the bad dream anymore, the bad dream that I was sick and sore and lonesome. I wanted to wake up and be in that *nice* place again.

But Mommy and Daddy need me.

I struggled to open my eyes.

By morning my temperature was closer to normal and my heart had slowed its erratic beat.

Dr. McPherson once again conferred with my mother. "She reminded me of a sacrificial lamb offering herself upon the altar. Lying there quietly. She wants to die. But I'll be damned if I'm going to let her! That little girl is going to live whether she wants to or not!" He slapped his large, beefy hand down hard on his desk for emphasis.

"Dr. McPherson said he thinks you want to die. Is that true?" my mother asked me a couple of days later.

"Yes."

"Why do you want to die, Korel? Is it because of the pain?"

"Yes."

"Oh, Korel, I know it hurts, but you've got to fight. You've got to live!"

"But I don't like this bad dream."

"I know it's like a bad dream right now, but you'll get better, you'll see. And what would Mommy and Daddy do without you? You're the only little girl we've got, you know."

29

THE DAYS TURNED into weeks and the weeks into months. I began viewing the hospital as home.

It's quiet here. I like quiet. Sometimes at home Mommy and Daddy have noisy plays. I don't like that. It scares me. I don't like it when they practise when I want to sleep. I don't like it when their bed squeaks and Mommy says, "No, Joe, no! Please no! You're hurting me." I don't like it neither when they turn on the record player really loud and people come. People are noisy and I can't sleep so I go in my closet. I like my closet. It's dark, and warm, and quiet. I like dark and quiet. I like the hospital because it's quiet. But I miss my closet, it's more dark.

People don't bring their kids here neither. Kids are noisy brats. They make me tired. They mess my room and I have to clean it again. One time Sharon even scribbled all over my bed with crayons. Cousin Arnie never does that, though.

I like Arnie.

I HAD LIKED Arnie from the moment I laid eyes on him. I had been three when my parents and I moved to the small Alberta town of Coaldale from Ontario, via rail. My Uncle Jack picked us up at the train station. We stayed with him and Aunt Kathy—Mom's sister—and their son, Arnie, who was the same age as me, for the next few days while Joe readied the house we had bought. Mom and Aunt Kathy had thought it would nice if we two children exchanged gifts when we met one another. So Mom bought a duck pull-toy for me to give to Arnie and Aunt Kathy bought a small rolling pin for Arnie to give to me.

He had stood on the porch, wearing white shoes and a white shirt, holding out the rolling pin to me. Arnie had an apple face with dark brown, nearly black, saucers for eyes that contrasted sharply with the blond hair that stuck up on the back of his head. He was short, shorter even than me. We struck an instant bond. Mom told me in later years that she had been surprised; I didn't normally care much for other kids. Perhaps, she had reasoned, we felt a kinship because we both came from single child families.

I like Arnie but I don't think Auntie Kathy does. Auntie Kathy is mean to Arnie. She's always giving him spankings with the belt because he gets his white shirt and white shoes dirty. I'm glad my Mommy doesn't do that to me. Auntie Kathy is nice to me, though. She says I'm such a good little girl. She says she wishes I was her *little girl.*

Everything hurt when I was at home because I was sick but I hurt here too. Dr. McPherson keeps cutting my legs by my pee-pee and by my feet. He said he has to do that so he can put a thing called a shunt in me. That's so he can put more blood and water in me so I won't be so sick. But it hurts. I liked it when I was really, really sick, though, 'cause then I didn't hurt no more. But Mommy and Daddy didn't. They cried. They didn't want me to die. They said if I died they'd be lonesome for me.

I like it here but I miss my Mommy and Daddy. I like it when they visit me.

DR. MCPHERSON GAVE ME an occasional pass and my parents would load me up—wheelchair and all—to spend the day or weekend with them. There were no "plays" or noisy gatherings anymore, and I enjoyed my time with them. Still, I tired easily and was happy when it was time to go "back home" to the hospital.

I became the pet of the children's ward. Most of the staff knew and liked me. They often commented on what a good little girl I was. They would say things like, "So tiny, yet so brave," or "She never complains." I soaked it all up and tried even harder to please, but I dreaded the penicillin shots in my buttocks. One time I covered my head, hoping that the "needle nurse" would go away. She didn't.

One day a new nurse came in who wasn't as impressed with me. My supper tray had been delivered and I was toying with a green vegetable with red flecks added, when she walked into my room.

"What is this stuff?" I asked her.

"That 'stuff,'" she said brusquely, "is beans."

My face reddened. I had known it was beans, I just wasn't sure what the bits of red were. I hadn't meant to be impudent when I used the word "stuff." I had been taught better than that. Children must always show respect towards adults, I knew. I wasn't sure what to say next, so I merely said, "Oh." I was glad I didn't see too much of her.

I really liked Dr. McPherson. He always took time to chat with me, telling me funny anecdotes that made me laugh and forget about my pains. Often, on my better days, he would take me on piggyback rides to visit other patients in the ward. One time he brought me a Cinderella colouring book and crayons.

There was a toy room on our ward that I visited on my good days—some days I was even able to walk now. Someone had made and donated building blocks to the hospital. While most of the girls enjoyed playing with the dolls, I preferred the blocks, making houses out of them. As there were plenty of blocks, I was also able to make rooms in the houses too.

I didn't mind most of the children in the hospital. Like me, they were too sick to be very rambunctious. There was one girl I especially took to, Pamela, who lived a few doors down from my room. She had lost all her hair. She said that she had something wrong with her blood. I told her I had trouble with my blood too—I didn't have enough of it. She was lonely. Her mother could only come and see her on the weekends. Pamela once told me, "Your mommy is so nice and she's so pretty."

"Maybe," I suggested to my mother, "when we get better, Pamela can come home with me and be my sister."

When she reminded me that Pamela already had a mother, I said, "But you're a better Mommy."

Sometimes I would hear Pamela cry because she was hurting. When I could, I would crawl out of bed and go to her room to help her forget for awhile.

"Don't cry," I consoled one day. "This is just a bad dream. Someday you will wake up and it won't hurt no more."

And then one night she did wake up.

I missed her.

I looked forward to my parents' visits, especially my mother's. In the mornings, my father would often drop her off at the hospital on his way to work and then pick her up again afterwards. From a ways off, I would hear the welcoming sound of Mommy's heels *click-click* in the hall, followed by her pretty face shortly after. Some days we'd draw pictures together, or she'd wheel me up and down the hall or walk with me if I was up to it. On the days when I felt poorly, she would sing to me. And after she left, I would cling to the scent of her Ben Hur perfume lingering in the air.

I WAS GIVEN a day pass for my fifth birthday. Mom decided to surprise me by inviting neighbourhood children and Arnie to join in the celebration.

To Mom, birthday parties were special. She remembered asking her mother for a party, year after year, and not being able to understand why her brothers and sisters could get one but not her. Grosma had told her it was because they were younger, but in later years she admitted that she just didn't like to host parties. She found the setting up and taking down tedious work and the celebration itself frivolous. She had grumbled every time she'd had to host one for the younger children.

Then, miraculously, a week before Mom's tenth birthday, Grosma had finally granted her permission to have a party on the condition that Mom do all the baking and other preparations herself.

My mother had readily agreed and set to work. Cutting out pictures from old catalogues and cards, she created colourful collage invitations and handed them out to her schoolmates Anna, Sarah, Gertrude and Rose.

The morning of her party, my mother made molasses cookies, gingerbread cookies, squares, and a carrot cake. While they baked, she took out red and green crepe paper left over from Christmas. By cutting the rolls horizontally, there was enough to string diagonally across the parlour from corner to corner. Periodically checking on her baking, she then began tidying the room. She put together the slumber bed, which she and four of her siblings slept on, toe-to-toe, each night, and covered its back with the day blanket—a rust and leaf-green afghan crocheted by her Grosma Bickert. Next, she folded her and her sisters' nightclothes, placing them in the dresser she and her mother had made. It consisted of two apple boxes, nailed one on top of the other, with shelves built in. They had papered it first with a layer of newspaper and allowed it to dry, then had applied a layer of blank paper, dyed yellow with a mixture of lime, hot water and the juice of boiled onion skins. A square of lemon-yellow checkered curtain covered the open end of the boxes.

By 1:00 all was ready. Then it had begun to snow, at first lightly, then more heavily. By 2:30, it was a full-blown blizzard. My mother lived ten miles from town. She knew there would be no one coming for her birthday that day.

MY MOTHER VOWED that when she had children of her own, they would have parties. Unfortunately, I didn't share her enthusiasm for socials. To me, they were noisy, chaotic affairs. I was therefore aghast when shortly after I arrived home kids began showing up at the door.

I retreated into my room. "I don't want them here," I whined, "I want them to go home."

"But Korel! They've come for your birthday. I invited them. It wouldn't be nice to send them all home without even a piece of cake now, would it? Please come out. Just for a little while?" Mom pleaded.

"Okay, Mommy," I sighed, not wanting to disappoint her.

Resigned to the inevitable, I opened my presents, politely thanking each guest in turn, and waited while they ate their cake and ice cream.

"Okay," I announced when they were finished, "You all got your cake, so now you can go home. But not you, Arnie. You can stay."

Mom, though embarrassed, honoured my wishes.

By evening I was exhausted and wanted to go back to the hospital.

ALL IN ALL, I spent two years in and out of hospital. During those two years, it was not unusual for my parents to be summoned with words such as, "You'd better come right away. It's her heart again. We don't know if she's going to make it." And sometimes while I was at home there would be an emergency rush back to the ward.

I came down with frequent bladder infections. It was determined that my urethra was too narrow. Using a series of gradually widening rods, and with much time and pain, Dr. McPherson managed to stretch it. I got ear infections—he handled that too. He removed my tonsils. Through it all, I continued to receive routine penicillin shots and vitamin B_{12}. Slowly my appetite returned to something close to normal.

Dr. McPherson recommended that I never have children. "Her body, her joints, her heart—all are damaged, and the strain of pregnancy and childbirth could prove to be too much for her. As you know, she's lucky just to be alive," he told my mother.

But I wasn't always quite as sick as I appeared to be. It didn't take me long to realize that when my heart acted up or when I developed a fever, Mommy and Daddy quickly lost all interest in their "play."

30

I LISTENED TO THE words of the song on the radio.

I saw Mommy kissing Santa Claus
underneath the mistletoe last night.
She didn't see me creep
down the stairs to have a peep.
She thought that I was tucked up
in my bedroom, fast asleep...

If that little boy's mommy is kissing Santa Claus and the daddy found out, he wouldn't laugh, he'd be mad. And that's not good. But what if Santa Claus is really that boy's daddy? Then the daddy wouldn't be mad, but that would mean there's no Santa Claus.

"I don't like that song!" I exclaimed angrily. Whenever I heard it after that I put my fingers in my ears.

By the time I was six and more or less recovered from my health problems, I had come to admit to myself that the violent arguments I often overheard weren't just an act. There was no "play" about them at all.

"Mommy," I'd scold my mother, "why don't you just listen to Daddy? If you just did as you were told, he wouldn't get so mad at you."

Still my heart hurt for her. Seeing her crying at the kitchen table one morning, I went up to her. *Poor Mommy is sad again.* Hugging her, I said, "Don't cry, Mommy. Life is just a dream. When you die, you wake up."

She sobbed even harder.

Later, after she had calmed down, I told her about the mysterious woman I had seen in the land of white.

"Mommy, remember that time when I was so sick? That first time?"

"Yes."

"Well, I went somewhere on a kind of merry-go-round and I saw a lady. I remember she was pretty but I can't remember what she looked like. But I remember she kind of looked like someone I've seen before. She was in this white place, kind of like a room or something, but it didn't have a floor or a ceiling or anything, not even a door. It was like a nothing place. Yeah, a nothing-but-everything place—a *nice* place. Anyway the lady told me things, lots of things. I can't remember it all. But I do remember one thing she said, 'Life is a dream and when you die, you wake up.' You know, like in that song "Row, Row, Row Your Boat?" 'Life is but a dream...' Who do you think that lady was, Mommy?

"I don't know, sweetheart. Maybe she was your guardian angel."

"But I didn't see any wings."

"Well, angels don't really have wings. People just draw them like that in pictures."

"Why?"

"Well, to show that angels can fly. But angels are magic. They fly without wings."

"Oh. Have you ever seen an angel, Mommy?"

"I'm not sure. One time when I was a little girl, I got lost. I was supposed to bring the cows home, but it suddenly started snowing and the wind blew so hard I could hardly see. I was so cold I couldn't walk anymore. Then suddenly two people came. They wore long brown robes..."

"What's a robe, Mommy?" I interrupted.

"It's kind of like a dress—well, maybe more like my housecoat, but you pull it over your head like a dress and it has a hood."

"You mean like Little Red Riding's hood."

"Yes. Like that.

"Oh. So then what happened?"

"Well, then these two people or angels picked me up and brought me into a log house. They told me I had frozen my legs and they started rubbing liniment on them."

"You mean like that stuff you rub on my legs when they ache?"

"Yes, that stuff. Anyway they rubbed them for awhile and then that's all I remember. Somehow I got home. Your Grosma and Bopa were very worried about my legs. I told them about the two people who had saved me. They didn't know who they could be because there were no log houses anywhere near us. So I sometimes think they might have been angels."

"Wow, Mommy! I bet they were."

31

DUE TO MY health, my schooling was delayed by a year so I was nearly seven when I started Grade 1. Because the nuns at school had been informed of my heart murmur, I received extra attention and privileges, such as being allowed to stay indoors during recess while the other children had to go outside. Since I didn't much care for most children anyway, I didn't feel deprived of play. I spent my respites reading.

My world revolved around adults—I lived to please them, and I became the pampered teacher's pet.

Adjoining the classroom was a small supply closet.

"Come to the supply room with me, Korel," Sister would say. "I need help bringing out a few things." In the closet, she would hand me a large piece of chocolate bar she kept there. "Shh. Don't tell the other students."

When I was four, I had weighed a mere twenty pounds. Since then I had nearly doubled my weight but I guess Sister figured I still needed some fattening up.

At home it was mostly my mother who was my playmate and companion. Together in the summer we'd lie on a blanket outside and look up at the clouds, spotting lambs or faces in them. At Christmas, the two of us would make homemade cards out of pictures and verses cut from the previous years', or we'd peel peanuts, looking for the "Santa" inside. She was my critic. If I was to be in a school play, Mom would be my audience while I rehearsed my part at home.

"No, that doesn't sound quite right, Korel," she'd say, "You need to put more expression on your face." Or, "Imagine that that's happening to you in real life."

Mom also coached me in singing and taught me how to hold my soprano voice steady so that she could slip in underneath in harmony. (She was eventually—when I was about ten—to accompany me on weekly trips via rail to Lethbridge where I sang on a televised talent show and caught the attention of Tommy Hunter. She received a letter from him; an invitation for me to sing on his show. All expenses—air fare, accommodations—would be paid for my mother and I. But Joe, worried I might grow up to be a "celebrity snob," vetoed the idea. And after that I refused to ever sing on the talent show again.)

Sometimes Mom and I just sat and chatted.

"Mommy," I said to her one day, "Sister Nunciata told us that Adam and Eve ate forbidden fruit. They gave in to temptation. That was called original sin. She said now we have to suffer because of what Adam and Eve did. Why would God do that to us? "

"Well, I guess it's because Adam and Eve didn't listen to God. They didn't obey Him."

"But that's not fair! If you or Daddy stole somebody's apples and I got a spanking for it, that wouldn't be fair."

"Hmm. I never thought of it that way, Korel. You're right. That doesn't seem fair, does it?"

"And did God put that tree there to tempt Eve? Did he put it there, then peek around the corner to see if she was picking his fruit?"

"No. I'm sure God wouldn't do something like that. What did Sister Nunciata say?"

"She says we've just got to have faith that whatever God does is good. But I want to know, if God is kind and good, why did he do that, and how come *we* have to pay?"

THAT NIGHT I HAD a dream. I was in the white world talking with the lady again. I couldn't see her, but I knew she was there and I could hear her. I had decided to call her Tutor, because Joe had once told me that a tutor was like a special just-for-you teacher. Tutor was giving me answers to the questions I had posed to my mother earlier that day—answers to those ones and much more.

I woke up the next morning, a Saturday, excited. "Mommy," I said, rushing into the kitchen, "I know the answer now. Tutor gave it to me."

"Answer to what, dear?"

"About God. She said. She said..." My mind went blank. "I know the answer. I know I do." I stomped my foot. "Oh, *why* can't I remember?"

"Korel, don't get so mad," Mom admonished me.

Joe walked into the room. "She's not mad. She's angry. Only the insane are mad. Now Korel, what's upsetting you?"

I scanned Joe. Every day I gauged my daddy's moods. I knew that when his eyes went big and black, or the corner of his top lip twitched, I had better be careful around him, and try to get Mommy to be, too.

Today his eyes were blue like the sky on a warm spring day—everything was okay.

"I dreamed something. I wanted to know something and then I dreamed about the answer, but now I can't remember it."

"That's because it's gone to a different part of your brain. The brain has many parts. When you are asleep, the part of the brain you are using now is turned off and another part is turned on. But when you are awake the opposite happens."

He paused in thought for a moment. "Come, I'll show you what I mean."

He led the way into the living room and turned on a radio he had recently fixed—people had come to realize he had a knack for anything electrical in nature and brought him their radios and televisions to repair.

"See," he said to me. "I have it on this station and you can hear the weather report, but when I turn the knob to a different station, what happens?"

"I can't hear the other one?"

"That's right, and that's how your brain works too. But sometimes, if you can get it just right like this," he turned the knob again, "somewhere between the two stations, you might catch a few of the words from both."

As I grew older and more able to understand, Joe would expound upon his theories. "The brain, like a radio," he would say, "is capable of receiving and transmitting. That's why, at times, you might get a phone call from someone you're thinking about or why two people sometimes think about the same thing at the same time."

He seemed to understand Einstein's theories and found it frustrating that so many others couldn't seem to grasp them. "If a person," he would say, "could surpass the speed of light, he would enter the past. And though light in this world," he would continue, "is a constant, time is not. You can validate that statement by comparing a mouse to an elephant. A mouse's metabolism is high; an elephant's is low. A mouse has to compress and slow down time to cram it into a lifespan of approximately one solar year. In comparison, an elephant must speed up and stretch time to fit into its sixty solar years. To the mouse, those sixty solar years would feel like thirty-six hundred years. To a mountain, it would be but a micro-second. Still another way to put it would be to say that the first seven years of a person's life are the approximate equivalent of his next seventy. In this example, his time clock ticks very slowly at first, then begins to accelerate."

Once you appreciated and understood the concept that time is plastic and light a constant, he explained, you could then begin to understand why surpassing the speed of light would put you into the past. Light travels at a velocity of one hundred and eighty-six thousand miles per second. Nothing in the known universe could surpass that speed. Time would be compressed to such a degree that the traveller would have no place to go but into the past.

It was only logical.

Joe was brilliant, but he made his living working in a brewery. In later years, I made the mistake of questioning him about this.

"Jesus Christ was a lowly carpenter," he roared in answer. "Am I to presume I am better than him?"

Years after that, I learned that Joe had tried to get a job in the field of science, but had been turned down because he had but a Grade 10 education.

32

I DAWDLED, SLOWLY MAKING my way to school, followed by my faithful string of admirers. Pausing by a snowbank, I began tearing off little bits of the bologna sandwich my mother had packed for me and handed them out to the cats and dogs vying for my attention.

Why, I wondered, *do humans think they're better than animals? Sure, maybe we're smarter, and we've got hands and two legs, but does that mean that people who are retarded or in wheelchairs aren't as good as the rest of us either?*

I buried the apple from my lunch kit in the snow. I liked hard, frozen apples and would eat this one later, on my way home from school.

I passed the large cage with the sign that read DANGER KEEP OUT. I went by it every day on my way to and from school. Daddy had said I was not to go near it because it could give me a bad shock and kill me.

I ambled on to school, placed my boots in the boot rack

and walked into the classroom. It was about an hour later that it suddenly hit me.

Danger Keep Out.

That's what it meant! God had a tree. It was dangerous. Adam and Eve had been told to stay away from it. Not because God wanted to tempt them, but because He was trying to protect them. But Adam and Eve didn't listen. And it was the fruit—not God—that had hurt them.

Thank you, Tutor! That must have been what you were trying to tell me in my dream. Thank you, Tutor. And thank you so much, God, too.

For me, finding answers to puzzling questions was the equivalent of a chocolate bar to most other children. I could hardly wait to share my discovery with my mother.

But, I now pondered, *how did the fruit hurt them and why is it* still *hurting us? What kind of fruit is it?*

WHEN I GOT home, my mother confronted me about the string of dogs and cats she had seen following me to school.

On a number of occasions, Sister Nunciata had phoned my mom, telling her I had been late for school or that I hadn't brought a lunch. Mom hadn't been able to figure it out. She always packed me a lunch and sent me out the door in plenty of time to get to school. So this morning she had decided to follow me from a distance and see what was going on.

"But Mommy," I protested, "they're hungry."

"I'll pack you an extra sandwich and you can feed them that," Mom relented, "but only on your way home from school, not on the way there."

"Thank you, I will. I love you, Mommy," I said, giving her a hug, "And guess what I remembered?"

33

KOREL, HELP ME, please!"

I ran to my mother's bedroom. She lay in bed, her face contorted in pain.

"What's the matter, Mommy?"

"I'm having a baby."

"A baby?" I asked excitedly. Visions of a baby brother or sister flashed through my head. "Wow! I'm going to get to be a big sister?"

For years my mommy had been promising me a little brother or sister and now I would finally get one.

I didn't realize that over those years, my mother had suffered one miscarriage after another. I just knew that she was sick a lot of times. This time when Mom had complained of cramps, Joe hadn't even bothered to take her to the hospital. He had angrily stomped out to his workshop instead.

"Can you go and get me a nice, thick towel from out of the bathroom?" she asked me.

I ran to do my mother's bidding and returned with the towel. She slipped it under her.

"Do you think it's a girl or a boy, Mommy?"

"Korel, Mommy's in a lot of pain right now. Please just hold my hand, okay?"

"Poor Mommy."

I stroked my mother's forehead. Sweat poured down her face. She gave a small cry.

At that point, Joe walked into the room. He peeked under the blanket.

"Korel, I'd like you to leave Mommy and Daddy alone for a bit, okay?" Joe said.

I looked at my mother.

"It's okay, dear," she said to me. "I'm all right now."

I walked out. Soon after, I saw Joe leave the room with something in his hand. He went downstairs to the bathroom.

Some unknown reason prompted me to follow.

I hid around the corner. I heard the toilet flush. When Joe left the room, I walked in. The toilet bowl lid was open. I looked in. The toilet hadn't flushed completely. In the waters lay the still body of my tiny, tiny, baby brother.

I decided I didn't want a brother or sister after all, which was just as well since Mom had a hysterectomy after that.

34

Sometimes it was hard to remember that life was just a dream. I was afraid to go to school in the mornings, afraid something might happen to my mother while I was gone. She had been to the hospital numerous times. The last time had been to have her goiter removed and she now wore a scar around her throat, like a necklace. Every day before I went to school, I would build an invisible, protective fence around her. I touched the walls, leaving my essence on them to help guard her while I was gone. I also thought about her throughout the day. About what she might be doing and where she might be so that the unexpected couldn't creep up and harm her.

I worried too about Joe's unpredictable moods. What if Daddy came home early and he was angry and I hadn't made the fence strong enough? If I was at home, I could usually protect Mommy. Mommy often didn't seem to notice when Daddy was in a bad mood. So I had to make sure I did.

I always knew. His face told me, his voice told me, the way he held his cup, tightly or not. Running his fingers through his hair or wiggling his foot were good omens. But sitting with his legs tight together meant a bad mood was coming. The worst of all was when his eyes turned black.

When he was angry, I tried very hard to make him happy.

Joe came in the house. I saw him take a slow, deep breath.

Uh-oh! Daddy's angry. My stomach started to hurt.

"So, did you miss me today, girls?" he asked, like it didn't matter.

But I knew it did. I ran up to him and gave him a hug. "Yes, Daddy!"

"Yes, Joe," Mommy said, placing a pot of soup on the table.

I didn't think she was really listening.

Joe sat down at the table.

"You know," Mom said, "they're hiring at the nursing home. And I was thinking about maybe applying."

"Oh. I see. So you're saying that you think I don't make enough money for you," Joe said. His upper lip twitched.

"No. No. That's not what I'm trying to say," Mommy sputtered. "I—I just figured with Korel in school, I could maybe..."

"Sneak off?" Joe's eyes were stormy grey. His mouth was pursed.

"No. No!" Mom cried angrily.

"It sounds like that to me."

"There you go again—twisting my words, changing my..."

I wanted to run, to hide in my closet. I wanted to cover my ears with my hands. I wanted to pretend they weren't really arguing. But I couldn't. I had to stay and stop them before my daddy started hitting, before my mommy got hurt.

"Daddy," I interposed, pasting a huge smile on my face, "guess what?"

"Just a minute, Korel, Mommy and Daddy are talking," he said tersely.

"But you're like Einstein," I quickly threw at him.

"What?" That got his attention.

"I told the teacher you know everything Einstein does."

"I, uh, wouldn't say that." His eyes slowly began to emerge from the dark pit into which they had fallen. "Uh, what did your teacher say about that?"

"She thinks you're pretty smart too, Daddy. She knows how you can fix radios and televisions."

"Well, I..." He ran his fingers through his hair, picked up his spoon and began to eat.

My mother opened her mouth as if to speak but closed it again when I nudged her under the table.

Later in the meal, Joe said, "I think you *should* go apply at the nursing home, Angelina. After all, Korel is older now."

Thank you, God. Thank you, Tutor.

For now all was well.

But sometimes I was caught off guard. There were times when Joe came home early and Mom and I hadn't heard his car in the driveway. On one occasion he caught us sitting at the table, laughing.

"How dare you laugh!" he roared. "I'm hard at work while you two sit and laugh?"

We quickly jumped up off our chairs.

He pounded his fist on the table. "You two don't even miss me when I'm at work, do you? You're glad I'm gone. That's why you were so happy, isn't it?"

"No, Daddy," I was quick to say. "We *do* miss you. That's why we were talking about you. We were laughing about that time you moved Uncle Jack's car and let him think someone had stolen it. That was so funny." I laughed, the words pouring out of my mouth without conscious thought.

"Yes," Mom agreed, instantly in on the act. "You really pulled the wool over his eyes that time."

Joe's dark expression melted; his face took on a boyish grin. "That *was* kind of funny wasn't it?"

Thank you, God. Thank you, Tutor. Thank you so much...

But there were times when both Mom and Joe simply ignored my peacekeeping efforts. Times when I felt terror hovering over me like a big black tornado. Times when I felt so alone and afraid.

God make them stop fighting. Please, God, please! I'll do anything you want, but please make them stop!

And sometimes Joe would start hitting Mom.

No. No. God, please, please help! Make Mommy be quiet. Make Daddy not mad anymore. Please, God, please!

I'd kneel in front of Joe, begging him to stop.

"Daddy. I love you. I love you. Please don't hit Mommy. Please."

Then he would suddenly come back from the dark place he had been in and pick me up, apologizing and promising never to hit my mommy again.

Thank you, God!

But sometimes I couldn't stop him. My pleas were ignored and I could do nothing but watch and pray.

God make it stop. Make it stop...

After such episodes, Joe would usually be in a good mood for a week or so, singing, whistling, joking, helping me with my homework or taking Mom out dancing. If the good spell was on a Sunday, he'd buy or make treats for the three of us to eat while watching *Bonanza* on television. Sometimes he would make banana splits by hollow-ing out cantaloupes and then refilling them with bananas, ice cream and the scooped out pieces of cantaloupe.

He was handy with his hands, not only with electronics and mechanics, but with carpentry as well—"It just takes common sense," he'd say. During one of his amiable moods he made my mother a round, tiered plant stand, and in another, he built me a desk.

But while he whistled and joked away, Mom was depressed and frustrated.

"Oh yeah, I'm supposed to be all happy and jolly now just because he is," she'd say to me. "I just can't take it anymore, Korel. One minute he's Dr. Jekyll, and the next, he's Mr. Hyde. Someday you and I are going to move far away from here where he can never find us, and we'll never have to be scared again. I'll find a job. And just think, Korel, we'll be able to sit in front of the TV and eat TV dinners as often as we like."

That was a special treat for the two of us since Joe always insisted on full-course dinners eaten at the table.

"And we'll have a deep freeze to put them all in."

Joe didn't believe in freezers either, insisting that they made women lazy, that once a woman had one, she wouldn't bother to can anymore—his mother had never needed a deep freeze, he said.

"And on weekends," Mom continued, "we could go to a movie or walk to the park and have a picnic like normal people do. Or, if we want, we can just...just do nothing at all. There will be no one to boss us. We won't have to be worried anymore that he might get mad about something. We can get a cat, too, like you've always wanted. Yes, life will be so good when that day comes."

I shared these dreams with my mother, but at the same time I worried about what might happen to Daddy if we left. I loved Mom, but I loved Joe too, and was concerned about his well-being as well as hers.

Mommy needs me but Daddy does too.

I never told Mom because I feared she'd see it as disloyalty. In my eyes, Joe wasn't an evil man. Moody and unpredictable, yes, but not depraved. I think on some level I thought of myself as the parent and my parents as two squabbling children I had to protect from each other.

35

"As you can see, Korel's marks are very good. She has an A+ in arithmetic, and she's at a Grade 6 level in reading and writing."

My parents were attending an interview with my new Grade 3 teacher, Mrs. Simpson, who had replaced Sister Nunciata for health reasons.

"I'm a little concerned, though," she continued. "I realize I'm new to this school and don't know Korel as well as most of the teachers here do. But I feel sometimes that Korel seems a little too serious for a child her age. She doesn't mingle with the other children. During recess and lunch hour she usually wanders off by herself to the far end of the playground and stays there until the bell rings. I've tried to get her involved in play with the other girls, but she doesn't show an interest. I realize she isn't as strong as the other children and must take care not to overexert herself, but..."

"Does she behave in class?" Joe asked, cutting her off.

"Oh, yes. She's very well behaved. A very sweet little girl."

At that comment, my mother beamed. She was proud I wasn't one of those types of children who, "screamed and hollered and made a scene."

"And you say her grades are good," Joe went on. "Then I see no problem. We send children to school to learn, not to play, Mrs. Simpson. If Korel prefers to keep to her own company during recess, I believe that's her prerogative."

But Mom didn't share Joe's opinion. The next day, when she and I were alone, she casually asked, "So how has school been lately? Do you like your new teacher?"

"I miss Sister Nunciata. She was nicer."

"Oh? What did she do that was nicer?"

"She let me stay inside at recess and lunchtime. Mrs. Simpson makes me go outside and it's boring out there. There's nothing to do."

"Don't you like *any* of the kids, Korel?"

"No. Kids are boring. They talk about boring things. They do boring things. They want to play stupid, games all the time, like hopscotch. It's so silly—drawing squares on a sidewalk and jumping over them. And the girls giggle all the time and cry all the time. Girls are always bawling about something."

"But there's nothing wrong with crying, dear. It's good to cry."

"I don't cry."

I hadn't cried since the day I saw my little brother floating in the toilet bowl.

My social life had always been an area of contention between Mom and me. And now that my cousin Arnie had moved away to Lethbridge, I didn't have anything to do with anyone my own age.

Nor could Mom understand my lack of interest in toys. What she would have given when she was little, she said, to have had dolls like I did. But I didn't care for them. Other than to place them neatly on my shelf like ornaments or display them on my bed, I ignored them.

"Who wants to play with dolls," I said. "They're even more boring than kids. I'm never going to have kids when I grow up."

"If you don't like kids, why do you like Arnie?" she had once asked.

"Because he's like my brother or something," I had answered. "He belongs here with us. Other kids don't. Other kids don't belong here at all. They belong in their own house."

My mother had given up trying to make sense of that last statement. So a little later she had tried a new tactic. "Well, you and a friend wouldn't have to play *here* all the time. You could sometimes play at her house."

"It's boring at other people's houses," I had grumbled.

TODAY A NEW thought came to my mother. "You like Arnie. Maybe it's because he's a boy. Why don't you try to make friends with some of the boys at school? I bet one of them might like to play with you. As long as they don't play too rough, your heart should be okay."

"They don't like me. They say I'm ugly."

"Oh, honey. They don't really think you're ugly. You're not ugly. That's just the way boys talk."

"No, they're right. I *am* ugly. I'm very ugly."

SPRING HAD ARRIVED and I sat under my favourite tree, an elm that towered far above the school. I often wished I could climb it and build a tree fort in one of its boughs. I'd bring up a blanket and a pillow and it would be like in the book *Swiss Family Robinson*—like living in a real jungle. But alas, it was just a wish. Such a thing would never be permitted. Even if it were, I couldn't. I had a heart murmur and was not supposed to overexert myself.

If this world, I reflected while sitting under the tree, is *a dream, then heaven, God, and Tutor must be in the* real *world. The Bible says Adam and Eve once lived with God in Paradise. So Paradise must be the real world. And that would mean that the dangerous, maybe poisonous, fruit must have put Adam and Eve to sleep, just like in* Sleeping Beauty. *And that's why we're all sleeping and dreaming too. But wait a minute... Adam and Eve would have died a long time ago, so they must be awake by now. I could wake up by dying too, just like I thought of doing in the hospital, but then I'd have to leave Mom and Dad and Snowball and I don't want to do that.*

That night I decided to pray about it. I had set up a small altar in my room with a statue of the sad Virgin Mary surrounded by candles. How horrible it must have been for her, I often thought, to see the soldiers come and kill her son. How would I feel if soldiers came and killed my mom or dad?

I lit the candles one by one then knelt in front of the altar. I made the sign of the cross—forehead to chest, left shoulder to right.

"Hail Mary, mother of God, pray for us sinners now and to the hour of our death," I prayed. "And please, Holy Mary, help us all wake up—Mom, Dad, Arnie, Snowball and me—all at the same time so we won't miss each other."

36

We were in the Rogers Pass in British Columbia, having arrived the evening before. Joe liked remote mountainous areas and, since we lived only an hour and a half's drive from the eastern edge of the Rockies, we went camping nearly every weekend and holiday from late spring until Labour Day.

We were exploring, Joe driving our 1950 Chevy station wagon along an old deserted logging road that slowly twisted and wound its way up the mountain. On either side peaks towered above us. The road narrowed into little more than a trail. Spruce branches slapped the sides of our car as we plowed on. The forest opened in patches, revealing deep, red-rock ravines through which white-water rapids raced far below.

Faint tracks led to an old log cabin long abandoned by the mountain man who had once lived in it. Such secret places hidden from the casual eye never failed to arouse my sense of adventure. This cabin was no exception. I went about, touching this and that, envisioning how it once must have been.

Here is the old pot-belly stove that the mountain man, tired from a long day of battling deep snow and bitter cold, warmed his hands by when he came home. And there is the can of beans he heated on the stove and hungrily consumed. The knife with the cold steel blade he used to open the can is on that shelf over there. And against the far wall is his cot where he lay at night listening to the howling wind, secure and thankful in the knowledge he was battened down in his warm, snug home. Oh, and over there is the magazine that he...

I picked it up. "Wow! Mom...Daddy! Look what I found! This magazine says 1949."

We flipped through the pages. Mom and Joe paid special attention to the advertisements. "I remember when things were that price," they remarked.

I went outside. Things were usually equally exciting outside the cabins. I saw a stable and a corral. Here the woodsman would have kept his horses—mustangs, I was sure—those tough mountain ponies that were so sure-footed they could "darn-near climb the sheer side of a cliff," according to author Louis L'Amour. Bays, chestnuts, blacks, pawing the earth, tossing their heads. I could almost smell their rich, pungent odour and hear the echoes of their wild neighing.

I had read a lot about horses, which, along with dogs and cats, were my favourite animals. Not that I had anything against other animals. There was even that time a couple of years earlier I had made friends with a bear...

We had been spending the night in a rented cabin. In the morning, awake early, I had gone outside and spotted a bear a few yards distant, rummaging through a garbage can. Thinking he looked hungry, I had gone back in and grabbed a piece of roast beef left over from the day before. The bear had certainly been amiable enough, even letting me stroke his thick, dark fur as he ate.

At that moment, Joe, who had just woken, had happened to glance out the window.

"Korel," he had called out to me in a soft, quiet voice, "I want you to slowly back away and come in here."

When I was halfway to the cabin, Joe had run out and carried me the rest of way in. I could feel his heart pounding. His face was white. He said, "Korel, don't ever feed a bear." There had been no ifs, ands, or buts...

I looked in the stable. Most of the tack was gone. There were no saddles or bridles—but there was an old rope left hanging on a rusty nail. I took it down.

I wish I could have a horse someday—an Arabian. Arabians—those loyal desert steeds that shared the tents of the Bedouins. How wonderful that must be! Your very own horse you could curl up with. You wouldn't be cold. You...

"Time to go, Korel," Joe's voice interrupted my reverie.

After exploring a few more logging roads and deserted log houses, we returned to the highway and drove a few miles, then turned down a gravel road that lead us to a campground a few miles off the beaten path. Joe always chose small, less popular campsites, and if anyone should set up in a vacant site next to us, Joe would usually have us pack up and move to a different spot. He liked his privacy.

After supper—complete with tablecloth and good dishes, also a must for Joe—we relaxed around the campfire, roasting marshmallows and singing. After a bit, Joe put his lips to his harmonica; he could play a mean mouth organ, especially the blues. He played a couple of Hank Williams tunes. He said he could relate to "Ol' Hank."

Then he put down his juice harp and began singing The Delmore Brothers' "Blues Stay Away From Me."

Years later, I can still see him sitting on that stump—his eyes closed, the firelight reflecting off his face—wailing in his jazzy tenor:

Well, I say, blu-ues, stay away from me.
Oh-oh, blu-ues, why don't you set me free?
I don't know why, you keep ahauntin' me.
Blu-ues, stay away from me.
Blu-ues, why don't you set me free?
Don't know why we never can agree.

Sunlight, diffused by an early morning drizzle, slowly crept through the window of the station wagon. I nestled deeper into my down-filled sleeping bag, leaving only my nose exposed. What a yummy sensation it was to have a cold nose while the rest of me was cocooned in exquisite warmth. It was like warming your insides with hot chocolate—or your backside by the fire—on a cold winter's day.

After a few minutes, the rain stopped and Joe emerged from the tent he shared with Mom. He began priming the pump on the Coleman stove.

I was glad my parents now slept in the tent, which Joe had bought that spring. Prior to the tent, all three of us slept in the station wagon, with me in the front seat and Mom and Joe in the back.

I hadn't liked the sounds my parents made in the night. I knew what they were doing, my mother had once explained it to me, but still the noises had bothered me. It gave me weird, mixed feelings—part sympathy, as I heard my mother's ragged whisper, "Joe, please no. Not tonight," part anger with both of them, and part something else I neither liked nor understood.

I rummaged through my suitcase and grabbed a set of clean clothes for the day, quickly dressing under the covers. By the time I emerged from the car, Joe had hot chocolate made. He handed one cup to me and carried the other two into the tent for Mom and himself.

In a bit, while my mother dressed, Joe started on breakfast. Though Mom was the one who made dinner, often on Joe's days off he prepared the morning meal. He now worked in a quick, orderly manner, slicing and frying bacon while the toast browned on wire racks. I was put in charge of buttering the toast and setting the picnic table. Joe started on the scrambled eggs, which were his specialty, making them to perfection: fluffy, yellow curds that melted in your mouth. The key to this, he stated, was to mix real cream in with the eggs, beat, pour into a pan with butter, not oil, and quickly fry and whisk just until set.

Later, while Mom cleaned up, I helped Joe disassemble and roll the tent. I didn't care for the job because he was meticulous about the whole procedure. After the bedding was removed, the floor of the tent had to be carefully swept. Any missed grains of sand, Joe said, could rub a hole into the canvas. Then the tent had to be folded, just so. He had shown me how to do it a number of times over the past couple of months, but it seemed I just could not get it quite right no matter how hard I tried.

And he would say, "How can you not figure it out? You're either an imbecile like your mother or you're lazy."

And I'd think, *Oh please, God, please help me get it right. Please!*

Once the tent was folded, we would tightly roll it, whisking as we went along to remove debris and moisture. I had problems doing that right too. I could never seem to get it to go straight on my end.

It seemed to me that there were a good many things in life that I just couldn't get right. Take, for instance, ironing day with Mom...

"No dear. I still see wrinkles." Mom would point out, flipping over the shirt I was ironing. "See, you pull it tight, like this."

I would try and try, but I just couldn't seem to be able to get every wrinkle. I'd get rid of one and then when I turned it over a new one would appear on that side.

"It's okay, dear," Mom would finally say, "I'll finish it."

I would breathe a sigh of relief. Why bother trying? I'll never be able to do as good a job as Mom does.

And then there was the time Joe had sent me out to burn the garbage...

I stood beside the burning barrel trying to light a match. With shaking hands I struck the wooden match against the box, but as soon as it ignited, I hastily dropped it.

"What's taking you so long?" I heard Joe holler from the doorway.

"Oh please, God," I whispered, "help me not to be such a chicken." I was terrified of fire. I tried again. It was useless. I just couldn't do it. I heard Joe coming.

Oh no! Now I'm in for it.

"You still haven't lit the garbage?" Joe bellowed, "I send you out to do a simple job and you can't do it?" He raised his fist.

I cowered.

"What is the matter with you? You act like I'm going to beat you. I'm not going to hit you." He grabbed a match and roughly formed my fingers around it. "You're just as slow as your mother is. Here's how you do it."

Holding my hand, Joe struck the tip of the match against its box. It lit. He directed the flame to a piece of paper and had me drop it into the incinerator.

"Now, what was so hard about that?"

"N-nothing, Daddy," I stammered.

"It bothers me that you cowered like that, Korel," he said. His words were drawn out. His voice became soft, and low—dangerously soft and low. "Why would you do that, Korel?"

I was scared you were going to hit me because I'm too stupid and scared to light a fire.

His black, cavernous eyes bored into mine. There was no escape. "Why would you cower as though you were afraid of me? Are you afraid of me, Korel?"

Say no. Say no. *"No, Daddy."*

"Don't I always treat you well?"

Say yes. Say yes. *"Yes, Daddy."*

His timbre began to change. "You know I only spank you when you're bad. Give Daddy a hug."

I did as I was bid. Thank you, God. Thank you, Tutor.

"Let's go in," he said, his voice now cheerful. "Mommy has supper ready."

Regardless of my failures, my mother always insisted I was very smart. My teachers claimed I was smart. But I knew better. I knew it only seemed that way. True, I was usually one of the first to raise my hand when a teacher wanted an answer, but that was usually because I had studied the lesson beforehand. When people were actually trying to tell me or show me how to do things, I often didn't understand. Sometimes it seemed as though their words came out too fast or their hands moved too fast. I had a voracious appetite for knowledge but I often had to read the material to obtain it. In that way, I could absorb it all at my own pace. I worked hard to hide my handicap from my teachers. I believed that if they and other adults realized I was, in reality, somewhat dim, they wouldn't like me anymore. Other than Joe, who suspected, Mom was the only adult to whom I had ever confessed this truth, but she refused to believe it.

Being inept in so many ways, there were times I wondered if by chance I had been adopted or...*maybe an alien ship crash-landed on Earth. The others died, but I survived. And Mom and Dad found me and adopted me like in* Superman.

I had further cause to wonder. Both my parents were stunning. Mom had long, golden blond hair that reached her waist. She wore it "Veronica" style, in a wave across the top of her forehead. That, she said, was the way the movie star, Veronica Lake, had worn it. Mom always took pride in her appearance. She wore a dress and high heels, even while camping. Everyone commented on my mother's looks: the kids in my class, hairdressers. Even strangers on the street turned around and stared.

And Mom not only looked nice, she *was* nice. She truly cared about people, she empathized with them and always took time to listen to their problems. With most people, if you said, for instance, that you'd had a rough day, they might reply with something like, "Yeah? Tell me about it. You know what *I* had to do today?" or "Gee, that's too bad." But not my mother. She would say, "Oh, I'm sorry to hear that! Come, sit down and tell me about it."

People were attracted to Mom like moths to a light. I was truly proud she was my mother, but I knew I could never, ever, in a million years, measure up to her, so I didn't bother to try.

Joe was a slim, good-looking man of medium height with thick, dark, curly hair that he wore "Elvis" fashion, with a thick ringlet down the centre of his forehead. That forehead was high and broad, a sign of intelligence, many said. Joe was a neat, tidy person who, like my mother, took pride in his appearance. He was able to paint a wall without getting a speck of paint on himself. He was addressed by many as "mister," and though he valued his privacy, he was charismatic—the life of any party. Joe was also the type of man who would give a ten-dollar bill to a homeless person and tell him to go and buy himself a meal without the guy even having to beg.

Together, my parents made a striking couple on the dance floor. People often gave them a standing ovation.

In contrast, I saw myself as homely. I had a mouthful of pointed teeth, an abnormality inherited from my Grandfather Bickert. They were my baby teeth and X-rays revealed that I did not have any adult roots. Someday, perhaps at the age of seventeen, the dentist informed my parents, I would have to have them replaced with dentures; the human jaw was not designed for fangs.

I had also been born devoid of fingernails and toenails, eyebrows and eyelashes—it was months before I grew any. I was also born with a couple of webbed toes. My mother said she believed that these defects were a result of all the X-rays she had been given when she was pregnant with me.

My platinum blond hair was bushy, resembling, I often thought, Albert Einstein's. Mom spent a lot of time fussing over it, trying to tame it, giving it hot oil treatments and curling it with rags, especially for Christmas concerts.

Why does she waste her time? I'll never look as pretty as her, no matter what she does.

Joe often came to my rescue with, "Leave the poor girl alone, Angelina, she's fine the way she is."

No, I was not attractive, charming, or smart—but I *was* proud of the fact that my parents, at least, were.

37

TENT ROLLED, WE loaded the car and started down the road in the general direction of home, stopping here and there along the way. Unlike many men, Joe was never in a hurry when we travelled. We reached Ainsworth Hot Springs by early afternoon. Ainsworth was one of my favourite places in the mountains. The resort town, located on the mid-west shoulder of Kootenay Lake, offered natural springs that bubbled up from deep in the earth to emerge in a cave.

I remembered my first time at the hot springs. I had been hesitant, uncertain. But then, safely ensconced on my daddy's back, I had overcome my fear. He had stepped into the mineral waters and waded into the cavern. I had quickly come to love the steamy, womb-like walls and warmth that had encased me and drove the rheumatic pains from my legs.

Today we stayed at the springs for a little over an hour before proceeding to Balfour, where we boarded the ferry that would take us to Highway 3A. I was always fascinated with the ferry ride across the Kootenay, thinking how amazing it was that you could sit in the car, for the full forty minutes if you wanted to, with the motor turned off, and still get to the other side. Of course, who would want to stay in the car when there were other things to do on board?

Mom and I headed for the little café on the ferry. It offered only simple cuisine such as soup and sandwiches, but Mom and I patronized it every time we came on the boat. There was something exciting, I always thought, about a floating restaurant. It was like a cruise ship sailing off to a tropical island. While Mom and I sat in the café, Joe usually stood by the ferry's railing and looked out over the waters.

After lunch, Mom strolled over to where Joe was standing. I usually found that open area to be too cold and windy—it made my ears and the muscles in my neck ache—so I spent the second half of the trip wandering around other parts of the ship. I read long familiar "warning" and "what to do in case of emergency" signs and my mind began to drift.

The boat is sinking. We all pile into a lifeboat and start rowing. The boat washes up onto an island where we are forced to spend the night. We look for matches. There are none. Korel comes to the rescue: she starts rubbing two sticks together and soon there is heat, blessed heat, for everyone.

I sauntered over to the engine room and stood by the door for a few minutes, listening to the ship's heartbeat. I had been in that room once, years earlier, when a friendly crewmember had shown me around. I still found the throbbing of the engines a little intimidating.

My next stop was the lavatory. I had a thing about bathrooms. Wherever we went, I always liked to check it out. When I was younger, I would decline eating at someone's house if they had a dirty washroom. In the bathroom, I would ask myself, "If I had to live in this small room, what would I do?" *Well, I could make a bed over there in the corner—or, if the room had one, the tub could be one. The counter could be my table and I could wash my dishes in the sink. And over there, in that corner, I could put the broom and dustpan.*

After my visit to the lavatory, I seated myself on a bench in the covered lounge overlooking the lake.

Before long it was time to go back to the car and we disembarked, hitting the road once more. We made a pit stop at the glass house, a house constructed of embalming bottles. A mortician with an eye for architecture had built it. Because the bottles were hollow, the air trapped inside made insulation unnecessary.

We travelled on a few more miles then paused long enough to pick a couple of gallon pails of cherries near the fruit-belt town of Creston.

On the homestretch near Fort McLeod, we spotted a family on the side of the road with the hood of the car up. Joe stopped and offered his help. With a little fiddling here and there, he got the car running again.

Mom said that was one thing she really admired about Joe—he was always there ready to offer his assistance when others needed help.

38

IN THE FALL of 1960 when I started Grade 4, a new girl came to my school. Jenny had a tomboyish look with a brown pixie cut and freckles. She was a congenial sort of person and it didn't take long for my schoolmates to accept her.

Jenny approached me one day as I sat sitting under the elm. "What you doing?" she asked.

"Sitting."

"Can I sit too?"

"I suppose," I replied laconically, hoping she'd get the hint and leave.

She didn't.

Maybe if I ignore her, she'll leave.

She continued sitting there. I was annoyed. Her presence was interfering with my daydreams. I sighed.

"There's swings and teeter-totters over by the other side of the school. And they play hopscotch and jump-rope by the sidewalk," I reminded her.

"I know," she said in a quiet voice.

Oh, brother!

"You live on a farm?" I asked for conversation's sake. I knew she didn't live in town. Like many of the kids, she took a school bus.

"Yes. We moved here in the summer."

"Oh. Do you have animals?"

"Yes. We have cows, chickens, horses..."

Horses? That caught my attention. "You have horses? Uh, what breed are they?"

"Dad says they're quarter horses."

"Ah, yes. Quarter horses, they can turn on a dime." I said knowledgeably, having once read it in a book. "Do you ride them lots?"

"Not much. I usually have too much work to do."

Silence followed once again. I felt uncomfortable, and still wished she would leave.

She asked, "Do you have brothers and sisters?"

"No."

"I do. I have a sister who's younger than me and I've got a baby brother."

The bell rang, calling us back to class.

JENNY BEGAN SEEKING out my company on a regular basis. I merely tolerated her at first but then, slowly, over time, I began warming up to the good-natured yet somewhat sober girl. I learned that Jenny had it hard at home, the way my poor mother had told me she'd been treated when she was growing up. She had to milk the cows every morning, help look after her siblings after school, and wash the dishes. On weekends, she had to clean the barn, and if she didn't do a good job, her father took a willow switch to her. I found myself thinking that maybe Jenny should come and live at my house so I could protect her.

I didn't talk about what went on at my own house nor did I view it as abuse, at least not consciously. I didn't question what might be mentally or emotionally wrong with Joe. It was just that sometimes he was in a bad mood and when he was, we had to be careful around him.

Jenny opened new horizons for me. Before, school had been merely a place where I went to learn. Recess and lunch breaks were times to be endured, not enjoyed. But now that I had a friend, I looked forward to these respites each day. Like me, Jenny wasn't interested in girly-girl activities like hopscotch or skipping. She liked to run and leap. I longed to do that too, but the doctor had forbade it. So Jenny and I mostly talked.

"There are lots of bad people in this world," I confided to her a month into our friendship.

I knew that throughout the world people mistreated other people and animals as well. A lot of people were just downright mean. I had heard about World War I and World War II, and about men like Hitler and Stalin, who had killed innocent people. Some people even fought over God. I had learned in school, for instance, that the Romans once threw Christians to the lions, and that later, Christian conquistadors had up and tortured and killed pagans. And it wasn't just in the olden days, it was now too, Joe told me. In Ireland there were bad Protestants and bad Catholics who wanted to kill each other. And Muslims and Jews in the Holy Land hated each other. And God was fed up with it all. It said in the Bible that a long time ago God had wanted to get rid of humans because there were so many evil ones. But some man talked him out of it.

"When we grow up, we should punish bad people," I groused to Jenny. "Make them pay."

"Yeah," Jenny agreed, "but how?"

"If I tell you a secret, will you promise not to tell?"

"Cross my heart and hope to die."

"Well, sometimes there's this lady or angel who tells me things. Her name is Tutor."

"That's a weird name."

"Yeah, well, it means special teacher. She told me that in real life I'm strong and someday nobody will be able to hurt me."

"In real life?"

"Yeah. None of this," I said with a sweep of my hand, "is real. It's just a dream. We're dreaming. See?"

"But it looks pretty real to me."

"All dreams seem real until you wake up."

"Yeah...I suppose," Jenny said, dubiously.

"While we're waiting to wake up we should make ourselves strong."

"How?"

"Well, I saw this show once about a big, beautiful, wild, black horse. He was a stallion. Boy, was he tough! He didn't let anybody beat *him* up. I could pretend I was him. His name was Black Fury, and you could be..."

"I know! Black Lightning," Jenny said, getting into the spirit of things.

"Now we've got to cut ourselves and mix our blood together."

"Cut ourselves? What for?"

"Well, I don't think it needs to be a big cut—just a little prick on the finger. It's because we've got to make this thing called a pact. That means we'll be friends forever, like sisters. Here, I've got a pin on my blouse, we can use that."

Rubbing our blood together, I said, "Now we've got to make rules."

"Why?"

"Because we're a herd and a herd is kind of like a club. Clubs always have rules. Our first rule should be: No crying."

"Why no crying?"

"Because horses don't cry, of course. Besides, crying is for sissies and we're not sissies. Right?"

"Right," Jenny agreed. "Who else is going to be in our herd?"

"No one."

"But herds don't only have two horses in them," Jenny noted.

I thought about this for a moment. "Well, okay, but only boys can join. Girls aren't tough enough."

I decided to set up a "class," complete with a report card to teach herd members horse language. "W-e-e" meant *Come here.* "H-e-e" was *Danger, stay back.* "M-e-e" meant *Fight.* I kept forgetting that Jenny actually knew more about real horses than I did. Maybe it was because she seemed to be quite content to go along with my ideas.

I also made a song to the tune of "Taps" that Jenny and I sang faithfully every day at lunch hour as we stood at attention with our hands at our foreheads in salute:

Fury, king of the plains,
wild and free, proud and royal, king of all kings,
monarch of all horses wild and tame.
Fury's king.

Though no one—other than Arnie when he was in town—joined our herd, we categorized everyone anyway. In our classroom there was Pamela who—with her long legs, dark hair, and olive complexion—was a bay Thoroughbred, while Vicky's pretty dished-in nose and flaxen mane gave her away as a palomino Arabian. Tall, rotund, hairy-armed Father Honan was, without a doubt, a blue roan Clydesdale, and Wilfred, with the runny nose, was a winded pony. Of course, Black Lightning, Flame (Arnie) and I were wild mustangs, born and bred.

I was not to overexert myself, Dr. McPherson had said, *But,* I reasoned, *this is all just a dream anyway, so what does it really matter?*

Boys would occasionally come over to where Jenny and I were playing, hoping to get a rise out of us. Their taunts fell on deaf ears. I now welcomed them. They were cowboys who had come to try and capture the great Fury and his band. Black Fury wasn't short or skinny. He didn't have a puffy blond mane and pointy teeth. Fury wasn't a girl with a weak heart. He was a *horse.* And not just any horse, mind—not some placid mare—but a wonderful, beautiful, wild, black stallion. *And if those ranchers weren't careful, he just might decide to bite them.*

The cowboys tried herding Fury, eventually knocking him to the ground, but the proud steed pulled himself up on his powerful haunches and faced his adversaries. His front hooves landed hard blows on the cowboy to the left. With long neck extended, he bit the ranch hand on the right.

His cohort, Black Lightning, got in on the fight, landing powerful kicks of her own.

"Boys! Leave those girls alone!"

Miss Clark!

"Are you all right, Korel?" The teacher inquired, concern on her face as she watched my heaving chest.

"Yes, Miss Clark," I panted, "I'm all right."

The teacher turned her attention to the "cowboys." "You

boys know better than to pick on girls! You know also that Korel has a weak heart. I want you to report to the principal's office at once!"

When the trio left, she said, "I want you girls to let me know if those boys ever pick on you again. All right?"

"Yes, Miss Clark," Jenny and I said in unison.

Darn, why did she have to come along and spoil all the fun? How are we ever going to get strong if we can't practise fighting?

After that, Jenny and I were more careful. We confined our activities—running, jumping and bucking—to the field beyond the playground.

At my next doctor's appointment, my parents were told there was an improvement in my health.

39

"MOM, GUESS WHAT we're taking in school?" I asked, walking through the door.

"I don't know. What?"

"We're learning about ancient Greece. Did you know that they had an army in Sparta and that when boys turned five years old, they took them away from their mothers and made them learn how to fight?"

"What a cruel thing for them to do!" my mother gasped.

"No. That's not cruel. It made them strong so that they could protect themselves when enemies came. They didn't turn into bawl babies."

"There's nothing wrong with crying, Korel," Mom insisted.

"And," I continued, ignoring her words, "the Greeks worshipped gods and goddesses. There was Zeus, the king of all the gods. He fell in love with a beautiful human woman, Europa. But he knew that if she saw him, she'd be frightened. So he turned himself into a bull. Europa saw the gentle bull and began petting him and then she climbed on his back. When she did that, he flew high into the sky and took her to a strange land. Then he turned back into his own self and told Europa he loved her and she said she loved him too. From then on that land was called Europe."

"That's a good story. Did Europa and Zeus get married?"

"I don't know, but there's another story, an even better one. Before there were animals and people, giants roamed the earth. Zeus told two of them, brothers, to make people and animals. They did and then one of the brothers, Prometheus, started giving different gifts to each animal. Some got wings, others got claws. He gave away so much stuff that he ran out of things when he came to people. So he went to heaven and stole some of Zeus' fire and gave that to people. That put humans ahead of the other animals. Zeus was so angry with the giant who did that, he tied him to a rock where he had to live forever, with birds pecking at him." I paused for effect.

"Oh my goodness, that's terrible," Mom obligingly said.

"But here's the really good part. Zeus sent a curse to Earth—a box with the first woman. Her name was Pandora, which means, 'a gift of all the gods.' He warned Pandora never to open the box, but she got curious. When she opened the lid, horrible things popped out, like sickness, hatred, pain and death. Things got so bad on Earth that all the gods and goddesses left. But one thing stayed in the box and that was hope, and because of that the goddess of innocence will one day return to Earth and there will be goodness on Earth again."

"That's quite a story!"

"Yes, and you know, I was thinking—Miss Clark said they're just myths, but it kind of sounds like it does in the Bible about Adam and Eve, doesn't it? Eve and Pandora were warned not to do something because it was dangerous. But they didn't listen...I think that whatever they did put them to sleep.... But anyway, both the Bible and the legend say that terrible things happened then. They seem almost like the same story, don't they?"

"Maybe they are the same story, Korel. Maybe it's like when someone tells you a story and you pass it on and the next person passes it on; it changes a bit but it's still the same story."

"Yeah. I bet you're right. The Bible called it a tree and the Greeks called it a box. Whatever it was, why would God keep such a horrible thing laying around?" I recalled the electric transformer in the cage. "God must have needed the tree or box for something or he would have got rid of it."

I grabbed a banana off the cupboard.

"Hey, I just thought of something else! If it's the same story, it's got to be the same God they're talking about, too. They must just call him by different names. Wow. I can barely wait to tell Jenny."

40

"YOUR MOTHER IS in the hospital." Joe announced as I walked into the house.

My heart stopped. Bracing myself, I asked, "Why?"

"She tried to kill herself."

My world crashed around me. My heart began to thud in my ears.

Life had been running on a fairly even keel for the past two weeks so I hadn't felt that familiar dread, that fear of what I might find when I came home after school. My first indication of possible trouble had been seeing Joe's car in the driveway.

"She might die, Korel," Joe said, starting to cry.

I reeled. Visions of my beloved, beautiful, gentle mother flashed through my head. *Keep calm. She'll be all right.*

"Aren't you going to say something?" he sobbed, "How can you just stand there, dry-eyed? Don't you love your mother? How can you be so cold?"

Life is a dream. It's all right. It's just a dream.

"What kind of a cold-hearted, reptilian creature are you?"

This is just a bad dream.

"I'm going back to the hospital. I'll be home later," he said, walking out the door.

"Rule number one," I choked as he backed out of the driveway. "Fury...will...not...cry!" I slapped my face and screamed out the words over and over again. "Fury will not cry! Fury will not cry..."

Snowball, concern flooding his brown eyes, anxiously nudged me.

When I had won supremacy over my tears, I gave myself a pat on the shoulder. "That's better. No tears now—good girl."

I knew that what had happened was my fault. I had been having so much fun today, going on the school field trip to the experimental farm near Lethbridge, learning about all those insects and spiders, and then chatting with Jenny on the bus back, that I hadn't thought of my mother even once. Now bad things had happened to Mom because of it.

If you worried about something bad happening, then it wouldn't, but if you didn't think about it, it would. It was part of the invisible fence that protected everyone I loved: Mom, Joe, Jenny and Arnie. I usually tried to keep the wall high and strong—especially for my mother—but today I had let it fall. The Evil One had been able to get through the hole and had hurt my mom.

I set to work. Joe had said that the human brain has immense power, that man only has to learn how to harness it. I concentrated, envisioning myself helping Mom sit up in the hospital bed and placing first her right foot, then the left on the floor, standing her up, and supporting her as she took one step, then two. I repeated this vision over and over again, until my head pounded.

Joe called two hours later. My mother was going to be all right but she would remain in the hospital for a few more days.

I did it! I did it! Brain power really does work! I made Mom live. Thank you, God. Thank you, Tutor!

Yes. Mom was okay for now, but I must never let myself be caught off guard like that again: her safety depended on it.

IN THE MORNING, I could hear Joe puttering around in the kitchen. I had to go to the bathroom but I didn't want him to know I was awake, so I stayed in bed.

Half an hour later, he poked his head through the door. "Korel, I'd like to talk to you, dear."

He came in and sat down on the edge of my bed. "I'm sorry. I shouldn't have said the things I did last night. That wasn't right of me. I'm just so worried about Mommy. She isn't mentally stable. That's why the doctor is keeping her in the hospital for a few more days. What she did, trying to end her life..." Joe began to sob. "That almost killed me. How could she do such a heartless thing to us? She knows how much we love her." He blew his nose into his handkerchief. "All she wants is pity. That's what it is, you know. I know you think I'm harsh with her sometimes, but you don't see the whole picture. You don't see what she's really like. People think she's so sweet, so innocent. They have no idea what I go through with her."

I wish he'd just leave. I don't like having to sit here and listen to him rave on and on about how horrible he thinks Mom is.

"I bet she tells you terrible things about me, doesn't she?"

"No, she doesn't say anything bad about you, Daddy."

I really had to pee. I began squirming.

"Well, I should let you get up." He rose. "You know not to discuss certain things with other people, right? Some things are just between you and me, our secret. Other people don't need to know."

"Yes, Daddy."

"I love you. Give Daddy a hug. I need a hug."

I did as I was bid.

"While you get dressed, Korel, I'll make us some scrambled eggs."

"Are we going to go visit Mom?" I asked later at the table.

"The doctor thinks it's best if we just let her rest today. I'll bring you to see her tomorrow."

After breakfast, Joe rolled up his sleeves and washed the dishes while I dried. Finishing up, he said, "See how little time this takes? Yet your mother keeps putting it off until she has a stack of them to wash. I've tried telling her over and over, but she just won't listen. It's sheer laziness on her part. That's why I get so angry with her."

I wish he'd just shut up. I felt guilty about letting him bad-mouth my mother. *But what am I supposed to do about it?*

"It's good you don't take after her."

The truth was I didn't like housework any more than my mother did. When I washed dishes—that is, when I washed dishes when Joe wasn't around—I dawdled and daydreamed, playing with the suds.

Joe poured some wine into a glass, downed it in a couple of swallows.

"I think today would be a good day for us to clean the car." Joe filled a bucket with hot, sudsy water. "Korel, you can bring out the rags, whiskbroom, and dustpan."

Outside, Joe began hosing the car's exterior. "I know your mother thinks I start all the arguments, but look how things are now. You and I aren't quarrelling; we get along. So obviously I can't be to blame for everything."

He turned off the hose. "How about you whisk the interior and I wash the outside?"

I would have much preferred to wash the car. I liked the feeling of the warm sun on my bare arms, enjoyed the slopping of the water, watching as it dripped unconcerned to the ground, and seeing the metal transform from dusty blue to bright cerulean. I did not like the task of sweeping the car floor. Joe was very particular: there must not be a particle of dirt left anywhere. Many people used a vacuum cleaner to handle the job, but he insisted that was the lazy man's approach.

"How are you doing?" Joe asked.

"Good, I think."

Joe peeked in and to my surprise stated that I had done a good job. I was even more amazed when, after rinsing and quickly drying the car, he said, "I think we're done." Joe usually insisted on waxing the car.

"How about we change and go to Lethbridge for some Chinese food?"

I wasn't hungry but getting away sounded like a good idea.

THE WAITRESS, PERHAPS in her twenties, with golden skin and medium-length black hair cut straight across her forehead, took our order.

"We'll have an order of chicken fried rice, sweet and sour ribs, and chicken chow mein. Oh, and we'll have Chinese tea also," Joe said, returning the menus.

"So, what do you and Mommy talk about when you're alone?" Joe asked when the waitress had gone.

"We talk about things I did in school mostly."

"Do you ever talk about me?"

I was wary. "Sometimes. We talk about all the nice things you do, like taking us camping, buying Mommy and me ice cream and chocolate bars, helping me with my homework, and going to my school plays."

"And Mommy says that too?" Joe asked.

"Oh, yes." I was thankful when I saw the waitress return with the plates of food.

"Daddy," I said, trying to change the subject, "what does infallible mean?"

"Infallible? It means free of error. Incapable of making mistakes. Why do you ask?"

"Father Honan came and talked as part of our catechism class the other day. He told us that the pope is infallible." Actually, I'd already known the meaning of the word because the priest had explained it.

"The pope infallible? No, that's wrong. No one is infallible, regardless of what Father says. Only God is infallible, Korel. Never accept anything as the truth just because someone says it's so, always question and think it through for yourself."

I pretended to think on that for a moment. "You're right, Daddy. Popes couldn't be infallible. I read that one of them, Pope Urban the second, ordered the crusaders to kill non-Christians. Surely God wouldn't tell the pope to do such a thing?"

"No. He would not. God is not prejudiced. It is of no concern to God whether you are Catholic, Protestant, Muslim, Jewish, or so-called pagan. They all worship God." He put a forkful of rice in his mouth. "You're ten now, Korel. I think you're old enough to go and experience different religions. Worshipping in the same faith every Sunday limits one's field of knowledge. Besides Catholic, there are United and Baptist churches and a Jehovah's Witness temple in town. Or I could drop you off at a Salvation Army meeting in the city sometime. Meanwhile, it would be worth your effort to look up religion in the encyclopedia. It should give you an idea of the various beliefs."

"All right, Daddy." I enjoyed conversing with Joe when he wasn't on one of his tangents.

But a couple of hours later, at home, Joe was back to carping about Mom. "She likes playing the role of martyr, you know, having people feel sorry for her. She even told the doctor that her attempted suicide was my fault. Fortunately, I was able to set him straight on that. My fault! She and I haven't had so much as one argument this past week. You must have noticed that?"

I had to admit that it was true.

"I think she just isn't happy when things run smoothly. She likes drama. As I said, she likes people feeling sorry for her."

An image came unbidden, a quick flash of a time I'd seen my mother crying on a friend's shoulder.

No, I must not think like that. It isn't true. Mom isn't like that. Oh Mommy, I wish you were home!

I felt a wave of—queasiness?—that I had been having off and on all day. I had experienced that strange, unpleasant sensation before, once, when I was very young and staying at Aunt Judy's house and then again in the hospital. It was an indescribable feeling that began in my belly and spread around to my lower back, something like an aching loneliness or longing and deep sorrow.

Was it fear as well?

No! The great Fury fears nothing! I admonished myself.

Joe poured a drink for himself.

"You know, when you get a little older, you and I will have to have a few drinks together, just father and daughter. Maybe when you're thirteen."

He swallowed the wine.

"She's always going on," he continued, "about how much she loves you. But would a mother who really loves her child try to kill herself? She would know that if she succeeded, her child would be alone, motherless in this world. Would a loving mother abandon her child like that? And if I were as terrible as she claims, why would she leave you with me? Would you, in her shoes? Think about it carefully, Korel, is that really love?"

I tried to block his words. *Shut up! Shut up! It isn't true. Mom* does *love me. She does.*

There was a knock on the door. It was Bernie, one of Joe's friends.

"Bernie, come in," Joe said congenially. "Sit down, sit down. I'll get you a drink."

I was free to go for now. "Thank you, God," I whispered.

41

I WAS SITTING ON the bed beside my mother, who was sipping a cup of tea. I had made it just the way Mom liked it, with a touch of milk. It was the first time since she had come home from the hospital that we had had a chance to be alone.

"Mom, why did you do it?"

"Oh, Korel. I just couldn't take it anymore. I had it all planned. I would take the pills and just fall asleep, and you could go live with your Aunt Kathy. She just adores you, you know. She always wanted a little girl. You would have had a happy life with her, not like here."

"Mom, I really like Aunt Kathy, but I *love* you. I want to be with you, not her."

"I just wanted you to be happy." Mom began to cry.

I put my arms around her. "Mom. I *am* happy, with *you*. Don't cry."

"How was your dad to you when I was in the hospital?"

"He was good. He took me out for Chinese food."

"Oh, that was nice of him."

"Mom, what happened? I mean, you took the pills but you're still alive."

Will Mom say a miracle happened? Does she realize it was me who saved her?

"It was the strangest thing. I took the pills and I was getting sleepy, and then I swear I saw your Grosma standing by my bed. She said, 'You get up right now and phone the operator. Tell her what you did.' You know I never argue with Grosma, so I did what she said. That's all I remember after that. I don't remember the ambulance."

"Did you see me in the hospital?"

Mom seemed a little puzzled by my question. "Well, yes, of course. You came to visit me there. Did you think I forgot?"

"No. I was just wondering that's all."

It wouldn't be wise to tell Mom what had *really* happened. It would be like getting the winning end of a wishbone: if you told someone what you wished for, it wouldn't come true. In this case, I could lose what had.

42

*F*URY STANDS VICTORIOUS *on the summit. The enemy, Englishmen from London, have captured Black Lightning and Snow Fire and placed cruel bearing reins on them—reins that forced their heads up, noble-looking regardless of how tired the poor horses were—just like in the book* Black Beauty.

But the villain hadn't reckoned on Fury.

Black Fury wasn't just any horse, not just some docile sway-backed gelding, but a powerful maverick. He had come to his herd's rescue, hammering at the pine log corral that encircled them. The wood splintered and broke under his iron-hard hooves. Then they were free!

Now Fury, with his strong teeth, tears the hateful leather off his followers' necks. They gallop to the sanctuary of the mountains, their long manes flowing. They...

"Korel, Jenny, suppertime," my mother's voice called from a distance, cutting through our flight of fantasy.

Jenny, Snowball and I climbed down the rocky precipice, raced across the grassy slope and trotted into camp for supper.

Jenny's parents had finally given her permission to go to the mountains with us for a weekend. We had been ecstatic. Jenny rarely got to go anywhere and this would be the first time she would see the mountains in person.

I had planned it all out in advance.

As we drew closer, I would point out, on the horizon, the faint impression of the Rockies. "See...there...what looks like low-lying clouds?"

"Yes," Jenny would say.

"Those are the mountains."

"Really? Those are the mountains? They look just like clouds."

"Yes, that's what they look like from a distance," I would answer with a smile.

As we began the slow ascent, Jenny would ask, "Are these the mountains?"

"Oh, no. These are just the foothills," I would explain. "They join up with the Rockies."

A few minutes later, near Lundbreck, I would say, "Okay, we're in them now."

Jenny hadn't disappointed me. She was just as impressed as I had hoped she would be. And just past the Lundbreck falls she had excitedly said, "Oh look there... water's coming out of that rock!"

"This is just the beginning," I'd said knowledgeably, "Wait until you see all the cliffs, and the waterfalls and..."

I was gleeful. It was I who had the privilege of showing Jenny the mountains for the first time. I was the one who had drunk in the look of amazement and excitement on her face as she tasted the majesty of towering peaks and raging rapids. The satisfaction I received from this was the biggest gift my friend could ever have given me.

The euphoria lasted until Sunday morning. Then reality set in. What had I done, allowing myself to be so happy? There would surely be a big price to pay—it was only a matter of time. Besides, how big a deal was it anyway? So what if I had been the first one to show her the mountains? What did that prove? My spirits plummeted.

I was quiet during the trip home.

43

MY PARENTS HAD another fight.

In the morning, Mom told me she would be going away for a couple of days.

"Not again," I moaned.

"Just for a couple of days," she repeated.

She left a note on the table:

Dear Joe,

Need to get away. Don't worry about me. I'll be back in a couple of days.

Love, Angelina

I knew Mom would be back. She had taken off before, after she and Joe had had a fight. She'd be gone a day or two and then return. Mom had asked me after the first time if Joe was good to me when she left and I had said that he was.

But what I hadn't mentioned was his syrupy friendliness. I didn't know how to explain that. Tell her that he's too nice, to the point that it makes me uncomfortable? I always dreaded her leaving.

When Mom ran away, there were rarely repercussions when she returned. It was almost as though the shoving and slaps she received prior to leaving were some type of advance payment she gave for a few days of freedom.

Maybe, I thought, *she's gone to see* him *again.*

One time, years earlier, she had run away, taking me with her. We had stayed in a hotel in Saskatoon. She'd met a man there she introduced to me as my Uncle Anton. I had liked him; he had made me laugh. We made funny faces at each other in the mirror and I had noticed that his eyes looked like mine—forest green around the outer edges fading to hazel near the pupil.

He had fed me pancakes; this was during the time when I still didn't much care for food. I remembered her asking me if I would like to have him for a daddy. I had answered that I liked him but I already had a daddy. She had cautioned me not to mention him to Joe.

I never did but I never forgot him.

Then, when I was nine, Mom had told me the truth. "Joe is not your real father. Remember the man in the hotel who fed you pancakes that time, Uncle Anton? *He* is your real father."

I had let her words bounce around in my head for a bit, tasting them. I'm not sure what type of reaction my mother had expected from me, but all I had said was, "Oh." I felt no excitement, no remorse, no anything. It was almost as though I had already known.

In hindsight, I wonder if she would have decided to live with him had I responded more eagerly.

Anton eventually married. Mom told me in later years that he had said that he just couldn't wait for her any longer.

44

I*T IS A GELID, ebony-black night. The brother and sister huddle closer under the buffalo robe in the buggy and shake the reins. Unable to see their way—thick fog blankets the Earth—they must place their trust in their mare, a pretty little bay Morgan, to find the way home.* Thud! *Something dark and ominous lands on the back of the wagon. The siblings hold their breath. "Meow," it says.*

Meow?

My cousin Arnie and I were sitting in the car waiting for my Mom and Joe, who were in a bar in the small town of Coleman.

It was common for Joe to stop for a couple of "snorts" at various hotels along the highway on the way home from camping trips while I sat in the car. When Arnie came with us, the wait for Mom and Joe was much less tedious and sometimes even fun.

Arnie and I were similar in age, three months apart, but that was where the likeness ended. Arnie, a gregarious boy, lacked for neither friends nor trouble. He disliked authority figures and was always being sent to the principal's office for one reason or another. He was also one of the few kids I liked. Arnie curbed the boredom in my life.

Waiting in the car on this occasion, our combined imaginations had transformed the cord on the back of the front seat, the one that all cars in those days seemed to have, into the reins of a buggy horse.

We had been doing just fine, "driving along" when we had heard the thud. Arnie's big brown eyes grew even rounder, if that was possible.

Then we heard the meow.

As one, we turned our heads towards the back windshield. On the trunk sat an orange kitten, three or four months old. Arnie reached out and pulled it in through the side window.

"Ahh, the poor little guy's cold," I remarked.

"How do you know it's a he?"

"Almost all orange tabbies are. It's rare that they are ever female. If they are, they are usually sterile."

"What's that?"

"They can't have babies."

The kitten was very friendly and obviously happy to be in a warm place. He purred and rubbed his body against us. His long fluffy tail tickled my nose.

"Let's take him home with us," Arnie suggested. Arnie was spending part of the summer at my place.

"How?" I said.

"We'll just hide him and keep him quiet."

I rather liked that idea and went along with it.

When we arrived home, Joe discovered the cat.

"It must have jumped through the window when Arnie and I went for that walk in Coleman," I said.

Joe, in an amiable mood, simply said, "Well, in the morning I want the two of you to find a home for him."

Come morning we went looking but though we went from door to door, no home became available. "Ah, Dad will probably let me keep him," Arnie said, unconcerned.

His father did end up letting him keep the kitten. Uncle Jack let Arnie do pretty much whatever he wanted to. Aunt Kathy had left them a year earlier and now Arnie was often left to his own devices. Although his father was good to him, Arnie saw little of him—Uncle Jack was a workaholic. A carpenter by trade, he worked from sunup to sundown, which is why, it was said, Aunt Kathy had left him. As for Arnie, she had figured a boy was best left with his father.

Joe offered to have Arnie come and live with us. Uncle Jack vetoed that idea but let Arnie stay with us on some holidays and for parts of the summer.

45

"NO. I DON'T WANT that thing in my mouth," Arnie yelped. "Get off of me."

I was sitting on Arnie's back in my yard. I had fashioned my own version of a spade bit, a painful bit once used to control unruly horses. Taking a pen casing to serve as the bit, I had glued green burrs from a Canadian thistle on it. A string threaded through served as reins. I was now attempting to coerce Arnie to put the bit in his mouth.

"You've got to buck me off, Flame."

Flame started bucking.

We horsed around for a few more minutes before deciding it was too hot for such antics.

"I know, why don't we set up a lemonade stand?" I suggested.

"Okay, and maybe we could sell a few other things too, things that we don't need," Arnie said.

We dragged a couple of old sawhorses out to the sidewalk and placed planks across to serve as a table.

Arnie put out old baseball gloves, a yo-yo, and a few agates. I contributed dolls. My definition of the word doll was: a gift that I don't like but receive from well-meaning people; a gift that clutters my room, making it more difficult to keep tidy.

Returning from the house with a tray of glasses for the lemonade, I came upon a sparrow. I set down the tray and picked up the bird. It lay cold and motionless in my hand.

"Poor little thing," I murmured, stroking the soft, dun-coloured feathers on its head. I brought it to the table and set it beside the other items for sale.

"What did you put that dead bird there for?" Arnie asked.

"How do you know it's dead?"

Arnie picked it up. "It's cold and stiff."

"That doesn't mean anything," I said.

Arnie stared at me for a moment with his large saucers, then shrugged. He had quit trying to win arguments with me years before.

Our first customer, a jolly man wearing paint-splattered clothes, came from across the street and ordered a glass of lemonade. The second, a teen with bobby socks, paused, glanced at the bird and hurried on.

Half an hour into the sale, a girl who looked to be a year or two younger than I stopped at the stand. Spotting the sparrow she asked, "Why is that dead bird on the table?"

"Maybe he isn't really dead," I answered, "Maybe he's just pretending to be. Maybe he's waiting for the right person to come along, the right person who can see that he's really a beautiful, yellow canary in disguise. Maybe he's a beautiful, magic bird waiting for a person with a pure heart."

"Oh, really? You think so?"

"Maybe. Don't know for sure."

"How much do you want for him?"

"Well, he might be worth a lot of money. How much do you have?'

"A quarter."

"Well, maybe you're the person he'll change for. If you want him, you can have him for that."

"You sold a dead bird," Arnie said incredulously when the girl was out of earshot.

"How do you know, for sure, he's dead?"

46

I AM STANDING AT *the base of a staircase in an old house. Dark and dingy, the chamber in front of me is alive with evil. An evil of such overwhelming magnitude that I can do naught but stand paralyzed with fear. The ominous, invisible force begins to close in on me.*

I woke up from the nightmare, the covers over my head. Afraid to move in case the evil presence might hear me, I took small shallow breaths. *Is it out there, hovering over my bed, waiting to pounce on me? Please, God, protect me.*

I lay listening, my eyes squeezed tightly shut. Time passed. I managed to summon up the courage to peek out of a corner of the blanket. *So far, so good.* I cautiously pulled the blanket back a little further.

There was nothing.

I had had nightmares before, but nothing this bad. I felt so helpless; there had been nowhere to run and nothing tangible to fight. The house had been alive with evil.

What did it mean? If life were indeed a dream, would

not then a nightmare be a part of the real world? But maybe a nightmare was a glimpse of hell. Maybe hell was where I would go when I woke up from this life.

I shuddered at the thought. I recalled Joe calling me a cold reptile. He had been angry when he said it, but still, was there maybe something he could see in me—something evil—that I couldn't?

But surely I wasn't wicked enough to go to hell, was I?

"Please, God, forgive me my sins," I hurriedly prayed, "I'll try to be better. I promise."

"No. You're not going to hell," Tutor's voice said in my head.

Though I couldn't recall in detail the land of white where Tutor resided, I knew it definitely wasn't hell.

I sighed a breath of relief and eventually drifted back to sleep.

IN THE MORNING, I told my mother about the nightmare.

"Did the house have a lot of rooms?" Mom asked.

"Well, it was big and old, like the spooky English mansions they show in movies. So it probably did have a lot of rooms."

"But you didn't see them?"

"No, just the big room at the bottom of the staircase."

Mom, sitting at the kitchen table, tightened the sash of her violet sateen housecoat. Unlike me, she liked to lounge a little in the morning before getting dressed. She poured more tea for herself and stirred in a dash of milk.

"Well, whenever I dream about a house with a lot of rooms, I get company. The more rooms, the more company. Was there mud? Was the house dirty?"

I thought for a moment. "I don't know, it was too dark to see."

"If it was dirty that would have been a bad sign. Hmm, did you see anybody?"

"No. There was just the house. But it wasn't an ordinary house, it was alive. It was a monster."

I absently stroked Snowball's head.

"I just don't know, I'm not sure what it could mean. I'll have to think on it."

My mother watched as I prepared to head out the door.

I donned my favourite sweater, a lemon-lime cotton button-up. It contrasted sharply with my cherry-red slacks.

Mom opened her mouth, then shut it.

I BEGAN MY trek to school. In the light of the day the dream didn't seem quite as ominous.

Perhaps, I reasoned, *a nightmare is simply a bad dream within this life-dream, a dreamer's bad dream.*

My thoughts turned towards the catechism class we had had the day before. We had been told that God had given us free will.

But was it, I wondered, *the will of a small child to starve in Africa?* No. But perhaps the child had been placed there so that someone else could be given the opportunity to grow by extending a hand to the child.

Well, that was all fine and dandy for the other person, but would a loving God really use an innocent child in that manner?

None of it made sense.

A sudden thought clicked in my head and I stopped in mid-stride. *But if we're all just dreaming, what does any of it matter anyway? If I'm dreaming, that means I made it all up. I made everybody up—Mom, Joe, Jenny, Arnie, the entire world! Not anyone or anything is real!*

The thought was profoundly disturbing.

I took notice of the flowers in a backyard garden. I passed this yard every day walking through the alley but I had never really paid it much heed. Now I did. There were tall hollyhocks in shades of pink, salmon, and crimson. Hugging the fence were sweet peas and morning glories, white ones, peach, mauve. High in a tree, crows cawed at me.

Am I really smart enough to make up all this?

Definitely not!

The ancient Greeks said that things had changed when Pandora opened the box. The Bible says we had to leave our home with God when Eve ate the forbidden fruit.

So that must mean that the world isn't *a dream—at least not* my *dream—but it must also mean that Earth isn't our real home. Is Earth a home away from home? Are we all originally from another planet?*

I must have somehow misunderstood what Tutor had been trying to tell me. Which, in turn, meant the dangerous tree had *not* put us to sleep. The truth, then, must be closer to the Greek "Pandora's box" version of the story. But that would imply that God was a cruel, heartless being, sending a curse to Earth like that.

I wasn't prepared to admit such a possibility.

And just who was the giant in the Greek story? Was he the Satan referred to in the Bible?

Questions swam around in my head. There had to be answers somewhere. I would do as my father suggested—look up different religions in the encyclopedia. And if I didn't find the answer there, I would go to the library. After all, the Bible said, "Seek and ye shall find."

As usual, I was late for school.

47

"I'M SORRY, KOREL, he was just too old. The vet had to put him to sleep."

There was genuine sorrow on Joe's face.

"He was suffering. But he's in heaven now," Mom said soothingly.

The blood rushed from my face. The breath was knocked out of my lungs.

This isn't really happening.

"What's for supper?" I headed to the kitchen, passing the broom on the way. I grabbed it. "My room is dirty. I think I'll go clean it."

Snowball.

"No, he's not dead. He's outside. See there's mud on the floor. He put it there. This floor is dirty. I'm going to wash the floor."

I set down the broom and headed for the mop.

"Korel," Mom said, reaching for me.

"No!" I evaded her touch.

"Leave her be, Angelina," Joe said.

I ran out into the backyard and crawled down the small path that wound its way through the thick caragana hedge. Hidden, I sat down, half expecting Snowball to come and sit beside me.

Snowball.

Tears came to my eyes. "No!" I reprimanded myself.

I wonder if Arnie is still coming over this weekend? We could walk downtown and maybe Snowball...

"Shut up! Shut up!" I began rocking myself.

"Fury does not cry."

Snowball used to...

"I said, 'Fury does not cry!' Do you understand me?" I slapped my face.

I rocked faster and faster. I rocked the image of Snowball out of my head.

Back in control but not yet strong enough to handle the look of sympathy I was certain I would find on my parents' faces, I remained where I was in the arms of the concealing jungle.

It was dark out when I heard the squeak of the screen door. Footsteps approached.

"Korel," Joe said gently, "it's getting late. You'd best come in now."

He waited while I made my way out of the bush. We walked together to the house in silence.

48

JOE DECIDED WE would move to the city, six miles away. He had received a good offer on the house and it would save the commute he had to make each day.

I was devastated. All that was familiar to me, everything I had known nearly all my life, was about to be left behind—my house, my room, the yard with its tall Manitoba maple and thick, dense wall of caragana.

I went for one last walk. I passed the theatre where Mom and I had once watched the heart-wrenching movie about the big yellow dog, *Old Yeller.*

I turned right and looked in the window of the drugstore from which I had lifted a comic book when I was six years old. My mother, discovering the theft, had made me return it. While I was on my way to the store, Mom phoned ahead to tell the proprietor what I had done and asking her to be stern with me. The woman later told my mother that she had done her best to appear angry but had found it difficult with "such a sweet little girl as Korel." But it worked—I never stole again.

I continued walking down Main Street until I reached the corner by the hardware store where Mom and I had always stood and watched the annual parade. I remembered one year a clown in the procession handed out candy. There were kids pushing and shoving each other, vying for his attention, but I had stood waiting off to one side. He had looked my way, passed by the other children and held out a handful of treats for me. "This is for you, little girl," he had said.

Making another right, I headed toward school, through the playground, and into the meadow beyond—the meadow with its thick, rich grass.

I wandered into the thicket of coyote willows.

For one last time, Black Fury walks in the dense forest that has over the years offered him and his fellow mustangs shelter from nature's cruel winds and biting cold. Following a foot trail, he descends the side of the escarpment to the canal from which he and his remuda have received sustenance when thirsty. Fury crosses the water to the other side and climbs the bank.

He whinnies a long, forlorn goodbye to his beloved home.

49

SINCE THERE WERE only three months left in my Grade 6 year, I went to the nearest school with an opening available, a small, decrepit, public elementary in Hardyville, a village within walking distance of Lethbridge.

The school had dark, sordid rooms and halls reminiscent of a Charles Dickens' novel. About the only thing I found tolerable about the whole place was its lack of plumbing. It still used an outhouse. This put me in mind of a campground.

I found the ways and thinking of the kids here to be alien. During recess, the girls stood together in clusters, talking about boys and fashion. They wore makeup and jeans and they giggled and gossiped.

The guys, congregating in their own circles, stood swearing and spitting and taking drags from communal cigarettes when the teachers weren't watching, which was frequent.

In my old school kids had still acted like kids.

I was miserable. I missed Jenny. I longed for my old playground—the trees, the plush green grass extending out beyond the fence, the stream running parallel to the schoolyard.

This field was hard-packed barren earth with a handful of determined weeds scattered here and there.

Fury could never live off this.

I kept to myself in my new environment, trying to remain as inconspicuous as possible. After a few half-hearted attempts towards friendship, the majority of the girls left me alone, but the boys were another matter.

"Hey. What's with that fuzzy hair of yours? Don't you ever comb it?" a boy remarked.

"Yeah," Another boy piped up, "did anyone ever tell you, you look like a witch?"

Spotting my teeth, the first bully taunted, "She looks more like a vampire to me."

"I'm not a vampire," I answered spontaneously, "I'm Black Fury."

"Who?" they asked.

"Black Fury."

"She means that horse on TV."

"Yeah...she kinda does look like a horse—a horse's ass!"

Laughter rang out.

Seething with rage, I attacked my nearest tormentor.

"Ooh. She wants to fight! Ouch! Watch out for her teeth!"

I kicked the next boy in the shins. The first one grabbed me from behind.

I struggled to free myself.

"Give?" the boy holding me asked.

"Never!"

Though too proud to show it, I was grateful when the bell rang, calling the students back to class.

Fury has been captured and is in the corral now, but one day he will escape and then he will free his herd and they will flee to the safety of the mountains. There they will remain for years in peace until his remuda reaches a fold of a thousand. Then the enemy will hunt them down and renew their attacks.

Fury will die nobly, defending his kind. He will sacrifice his life so that the others may live. Released from the confines of the flesh, Fury will then be able to obtain a greater power and he will slay the adversary, thereby bringing peace once more to the Earth.

50

A COUPLE OF WEEKS after moving into my new school, I warmed up to one of the girls, Alice. She didn't seem to be as much into fashion and gossiping as the rest of the girls were. After school one day she invited me to her house, which was only a couple of blocks away.

The first thing that caught my attention was how tidy her house was. The floor was clean and no dirty dishes sat in the sink. My gaze took in sheets that were neatly pinned over the windows.

What a great idea, I thought.

At home we had to wash our lacy curtains by hand in the bathtub. With these, all you would have to do was throw them in the washing machine. I also took note of the wooden apple boxes equipped with little shelves posing as cupboards. *Smart, very smart.* On cleaning day, you only need empty them, give them a few taps outside to loosen the dust, then put everything back in. So much simpler than real cupboards.

Alice set a frying pan on the stove. "Would you like a snack?" she asked.

"AND SHE HAS an outhouse, like in a campground," I explained to my mother when I got back home. "I wish *we* had an outhouse. What do we really need a flush toilet for anyway? Something else, Alice made me this yummy fried bread. She puts lard in a frying pan, waits until it's hot, then puts slices of bread in it. She fries it until it's crispy brown. It's just *s-o-o* good. I'm going to make some. Would you like a slice?"

Mom, who had been quietly listening to all the merits of Alice's home, said thank you but no, she had had her fill of lard sandwiches when she was growing up.

One Sunday afternoon, Alice gave me a call and asked if I'd like to come over. When I arrived, a couple of her other friends were visiting as well. The four of us sat outside in the yard enjoying the warm spring air. There was some whispering between Alice's other two buddies. They went together into the outhouse. They were in there for awhile. When they emerged, Alice grabbed my hand and said, "Let's you and I go in."

"But I don't have to go," I said.

"Not to pee," she whispered. "Let's play you look at mine and I'll look at yours. Do you want to?"

"I um...I just remembered that Dad said I had to be home by three and it's already past that. I've got to get going."

I walked home at a rapid pace. As soon as I got through the door I told Mom what had happened, and she agreed that she would have wanted to leave quickly too.

I never went to Alice's house again after that.

THERE WAS A boy who went to the village school who, like me, lived in Lethbridge.

Unlike most of the guys, he was nice to me. He asked me one day after school if I would mind if he walked home with me. I told him that I wouldn't mind.

I needed to use the outhouse but was too shy to tell him that. It was a mile-long walk to my house but I figured I could hold it that long. A few minutes into the walk, it began to rain and then I really had to go bad. Unfortunately, there were no hidden places where I could relieve myself.

Then, to my horror, I felt it.

He must have noticed the sudden despair on my face, for he glanced down then quickly looked away, pretending he hadn't seen the rapidly spreading dampness on my pants. He said not a word to anyone about the episode, but I was too mortified to ever speak to him again.

51

SIX WEEKS BEFORE the end of the school year, my parents were called in for an interview with the teacher.

"Frankly," he said, "if it weren't for the marks forwarded to me from Korel's previous school, I would be inclined to believe she's backward. She can't seem to grasp anything I try to teach her. She gets into fights with the boys and snubs the girls. Please don't take offence, but have you ever considered having her evaluated by a psychiatrist?"

Joe looked at the teacher coldly. "My daughter is not an imbecile nor is she mad. If she isn't learning, I would suggest you take a good look at your capabilities as a teacher."

I TOOK ONE look at my father's face as he walked in the door and knew I was in trouble.

He grabbed me by the arm.

"Do you know that your teacher thinks you're insane?"

He shook me. "He thinks you're an imbecile, that you're backward. Get over that chair."

"No, Daddy. Please."

"I said, get over that chair and pull down your pants." My father undid the buckle of his belt. "No child of mine is backward."

The belt made a resounding *whack* as it landed on my bare buttocks. I winced as I felt its heat.

Rule #1: Fury does not cry.

Whap! The belt grazed my upper thigh.

Rule #2: No whip can break Fury's spirit.

Whack!

No crying!

Whap!

"He says you're backward. But we know better, don't we? You're just lazy, right?"

Whack!

"Yes," I answered through clenched teeth.

Whap!

"Louder!"

Whap!

"Yes."

Whap!

Fury will not cry!

Whack! Whack!

"Joe! That's enough," I heard my mother say, "Have you gone crazy? Her bum is bleeding!"

"You! *You* dare call me mad!" My father spun around and struck Mom's face with the belt. "This is all *your* fault, isn't it? If she's dim, it's your fault! Whoring around with a retard."

He punched her. A bottom tooth split her lip. Instant red sprouted from her mouth.

"No! Joe! No!" she screamed, shielding her face with her arms.

I sprang off the chair, raced to my mother's side and knelt in front of my father. "No! Please don't hurt Mommy! You're right. I've been lazy. I'll do better. I promise. I'll work hard. I'll be a good girl."

My father lowered his fist. "You'll improve your grades?"

"Yes, Daddy."

"Then go to your room and study and stay there until I say you can come out. And from now on you will wear dresses to school. Do you hear me?"

"Yes, Daddy."

"You're a girl and you'll start dressing like one."

I SAT AT the desk in my room. My bottom was sore. But that was all right, it would toughen me up, just like it had hardened the kids back in ancient Sparta. I figured I deserved a belting, but not for the reasons he stated, and certainly not from him.

The reason I deserved disciplinary action was because I had let down my guard and now the secret had been exposed—the truth—that I was inferior in intelligence, that I was dim. I had known for years that when people tried to explain things to me I often couldn't comprehend. My brain seemed to move more slowly than others' did. But I had worked hard to hide my handicap. I tried to nod, shake my head, or make appropriate facial expressions in the right places when a teacher or other adult talked.

Each day, I would bring the schoolbooks home, read them and in that way learn what the teacher was saying. With books, speed was not a necessity. I could learn at my own pace. I had never been concerned that others might think of me as stupid, for I knew they didn't. What had worried me was that someday someone would come to realize that I was.

And now someone had.

This teacher in my new school, obviously more observant than my previous ones, must have noticed my difficulties. And I had become careless, allowed myself to get too lost in my daydreams, had failed to nod or shake my head when I should have or make sufficient eye contact with my teacher, and it was for that I deserved chastisement.

Joe, the man I called father, had been the administrator of blows I deserved—not for being lazy as he thought—but for being lax in my vigilance. Still, it wasn't his place to discipline me for my mistake; it was mine.

It reminded me of a Bible story I had once heard in church. A man had made a transgression and God smote him for it. The man was going to punish himself as well, but God had forbidden him to do it. I had felt anger with God when I heard the story. How dare God take away that man's right to discipline himself? I now felt that same anger with Joe.

THE NEXT AFTERNOON, a Saturday, Joe walked into my room. "I can see you've really been studying hard. That's good. How would you like to take a break and go for a burger and fries with Mommy and me?"

"No thank you, Daddy. You're right. I need to study more."

"Honey, when I said you had to study, I didn't mean you couldn't take any breaks."

I hate you!

"That's okay, Daddy. I don't want to be lazy anymore."

"I'm sorry I had to spank you so hard. I just want you to grow up to be a good girl. You understand, don't you?

"Of course, Daddy."

I understand you're trying to break the great Black Fury.

"Mommy informed me that you're not treated very well in this school. So next year I'm enrolling you in a different school, a better one. Come on. Give Daddy a hug."

I obediently did as I was bid.

Hate fills Fury's soul, hatred for his captor, for this common enemy who took the whip to him and to one of his herd and then turned around and expected all to be forgiven.

It was like that Bible story I had remembered the previous day. God had hurt the man and then turned around and suddenly decided to be nice.

"Let Daddy buy you something to eat."

"I'm not really hungry, Daddy, I want to stay here and study some more. You and Mommy go."

Joe looked crestfallen as he left the room.

Now it's his turn to suffer, I thought gleefully. *Fury isn't about to eat his captor's oats. He'd rather starve.*

An hour later, Joe returned with a burger and a chocolate milkshake in his hands. "For my little girl," he said, handing them to me.

"Thank you, Daddy," I said politely.

Look at the worm squirm.

"Well, eat."

"In a minute, Daddy." Setting the food on my desk, I pretended to turn my attention back to my notebook. "I want to be a good girl for you. I've got a lot of catching up to do on my schoolwork."

Seeing his pain, so much tastier than eating his oats.

Joe left the room, returning half an hour later. "Sweetheart, you didn't touch your burger," he said.

"Oh! You're right. I'm so sorry, Daddy. I really did appreciate what you brought me but I've been so busy doing this essay, I forgot all about it."

Suffer and squirm, Joe.

Five minutes after Joe walked out Mom came in. "Korel, he really is sorry. He feels terrible. Please come out of your room."

"No!"

"Please. At least eat what he brought you."

"No."

"But you haven't eaten anything since yesterday! Please. Do it for me."

I looked at her. I looked at her lip still swollen from yesterday. "Why do you let him do that, Mom? Why do you let him be nice to you after he's hit you?"

"Someday you'll understand, dear."

"I'll never understand," I said with venom in my voice.

I FELT ANGER towards my mother; I felt betrayed. Within a week, however, I too was taking pity upon Joe, succumbing to his charms. Then he turned ugly again and how I hated him.

But above all, I despised myself, spat on myself for having been such a fool, for being weak like my mother. I wished he would just stay mean. At times, I found myself wishing he would just beat me every day, beat the hate in deeper and deeper.

Scar Fury's back. Make him stronger.

Life would be so much easier that way.

52

TRUE TO HIS word, Joe sent me to a better school in the fall. Unfortunately, my reputation followed me, as one of my former classmates was a friend of a student here.

One day after class a couple of boys cornered me.

"So. I hear you think you're a horse," one of them said, "that you like to fight."

I tried to turn a deaf ear. *The great stallion was tired, having grown weary of fighting.*

"I hear you think you're tough," the boy persisted.

"She don't look so tough to me," his companion gibed.

"Leave her alone," a third voice cut in.

We turned to look at the newcomer—a freckled boy I recognized from my class.

"Wanna make me?" the first boy asked.

"Sure," Freckles said, stepping forward.

I didn't know that my defender had won kickboxing

awards, but it was common knowledge to the rest of my class.

"Hey. We were just kiddin'," the second boy said, backing away.

"Ah, yeah," the first said, joining him.

Shifting his attention to me, Freckles, whose real name turned out to be Bobby, asked me, "Could I walk you home?"

"Okay," I answered, shyly. I felt perspiration on the palms of my hands. Mean boys I could deal with, but nice ones made me nervous. I frantically searched my mind for something to say.

Thank you for sticking up for me? No. That would make me look like a girly-girl who couldn't defend herself.

"Do you like cats?" Bobby asked.

"Yes. I love animals."

"Well, my cat had a litter of kittens. Would you like one?"

"I'd have to ask my dad."

"Well, if he says yes, you could walk home with me tomorrow after school and pick one out."

"Thank you," I said, smiling.

JOE, IN GOOD spirits, gave his permission and the following day I walked with Bobby to his house.

"So, who's your friend?" Bobby's mother asked when we walked in the door.

"This is Korel," he answered.

I felt awkward. I didn't know Bobby's surname so wasn't sure how to address his mother.

"Pleased to meet you, ma'am," was what I said.

A look of surprise came over the woman's face but, quickly recovering, she smiled and said, "Well, I'm very pleased to meet you too, Korel. Don't mind my son's manners. My name is Grace."

"Come on," Bobby said, "I'll show you the kittens."

Weaving his way around scattered toys, he led the way into the living room, passing an overturned laundry basket near a sofa overflowing with unfolded clothes, and a coffee table cluttered with books and magazines before finally coming to a door leading to the basement. Bobby made a pathway for me down stairs littered with dirty laundry.

"Here they are," he said, walking up to a box tucked away under a bench.

"Oh! They're so cute!" I exclaimed, stroking their warm, furry bodies.

A little grey and white male particularly caught my attention. Nuzzling up to my hand, he began licking it.

"I think I like this one the best," I said.

"Hey. Who's your friend?" a voice behind me asked.

I turned and saw a girl I recognized from school.

"Oh. I know you. You're the new girl in my class. Korel, right?"

"This is my twin sister, Suzie," Bobby announced.

"You like cats too?" Suzie asked me.

"Yes. I do."

"She's going to take one of the kittens," Bobby said.

"Oh, good. I'm glad. Mom and Dad said that we've got to find homes for all of them...Hey!" she suddenly announced, "*Mr. Ed* is on."

Strains of the show's opening song blared above us on the television: *A horse is a horse, of course, of course, and no one can talk to a horse, of course. That is, of course, unless the horse is the famous Mr. Ed.*

"Last one up the stairs is a rotten egg," Suzie threw at us halfway up.

Hastily throwing the clean laundry back into the basket, Bobby made a spot for me to sit on the sofa while

Suzie and her two other brothers scrambled for seats of their own.

So began a couple of new friendships for me.

Phantom, the little tom I had picked out, also became a good friend. He kept me company on trips to the mountains. Now that I was a preteen, I had begun to find the frequent forays monotonous.

But I had infinite patience with Phantom. I bought him a leash and collar and taught him to heel like a dog, then took him on walks downtown. People turned and stared and I received a lot of comments; they had never seen someone walk a cat before. For a year, Phantom and I were almost inseparable and then one day he vanished. Mom believed someone, noticing his talents, had likely stolen him.

53

THE FIRST TIME Suzie came to visit she gazed in wonder at my room. In it sat my own jukebox and desk that Joe had made for me.

"Boy, you're so lucky," Suzie said enviously. "I wish I had a life like yours. I've got to share everything with my brothers all the time."

I didn't discuss what went on at my house with Suzie and Bobby. Aside from viewing it as a disloyalty to my parents, I knew it was something my friends would just never understand. I said merely that my father was strict.

I preferred to visit the twins at their house. Though cluttered, their home was warm, friendly and fun. The kids, a noisy lot, didn't stiffen when their father came home, as I did. I thought Mr. Benard was nice, but Joe didn't care for him. Joe said he was a scab because he had broken the picket line during a recent strike at the brewery where they both worked.

Joe was a strong believer in the workers' union. "Before

unions came into being, companies could get away with just about anything," he explained to me. "Poor working conditions, long hours for little pay. If a worker complained, he was told he could go find a different job, and a man willing to take his place was hired. Unions won't let employers get away with that, they protect the labourer. Now when a company won't listen to its workers' requests, the union brings on a strike. That means the men refuse to work and they form a picket line until an agreement is reached. Men who break the picket, who go to work..." Joe grew hot under the collar just talking about it, "...are scabs. They have no vision or thought for the future. They have no concern for others. They think only of themselves."

Suzie also brought up the subject of the strike to me. "Everyone's mad at my dad because he broke the picket line, but he did it because he loves us." Suzie held her head up proudly. "He says the heck with the union—he's got a family to feed and when you go on strike, you lose money."

I didn't say anything. I didn't tell her what Joe had said. I could see both sides.

Mom hosted a large party for my thirteenth birthday, inviting my entire seventh grade class. Beforehand she took me to the thrift store and helped me pick out a dress. The dress we chose, a pink one, was a little too long and big around the waist. My mother wasn't daunted. She said she could fix it and she did. With a touch here and there, and some lace and ribbon she remodelled it into a princess-style gown.

She also brought me to a salon to have my hair cut and styled. She was so excited for me. I had never had my hair done by a professional before and she was sure I'd look gorgeous when the hairdresser was done with me. Her optimism was contagious. I grew excited as well—I would finally be pretty.

But when the beautician was finished and I looked in the mirror, I felt like bawling my eyes out. My fine hair, usually curly and frizzy, was now straight and frizzy. The woman hadn't tamed my hair; she had killed it. Instead of a live tumbleweed, it was now a dead, flattened one.

But Mom went on about how lovely she thought I looked.

I was angry with her. I wanted to scream at her, *Why are you saying that? You know I look horrible! Why did you bring me here? Why? All you did was build up my hopes for nothing. No one can make me look pretty. No one!*

But instead I smiled. I couldn't hurt Mom. She had tried. She had been so sure they could work magic and she had paid good money just for me. It wasn't her fault it didn't work.

I had to get out of there. I felt like I couldn't breathe, as though I was going to suffocate. I politely thanked the hairdresser, then hurried Mom out.

Mom and I set up balloons and streamers in the living room. When Bobby and Arnie arrived, she solicited their help in moving the furniture against the wall to make room for dancing.

The girls at my party complimented me on my dress and hair.

They're just trying to make me feel good. I know how horrible I look.

Mom flitted from one guest to the next. She approached Sarah, a shy girl with a bad case of acne. "I can't help but notice you have the most beautiful blue eyes, Sarah. They are absolutely gorgeous."

Sarah's face lit up at Mom's words. "Thank you, Mrs. Jaslo."

Mom spotted a boy standing alone in the corner. “Come dance with me. Your name is Tom, right?” Mom expertly guided him across the floor, ignoring his fumbling steps. By the end of the dance he was noticeably more relaxed.

Suzie was impressed with the party. “Your mother is so pretty and cool. I wish I had a Mom like yours.”

The other girls, and even the boys, echoed her sentiments. “She’s so nice to talk to.”

I beamed, proud of my mother.

54

I WAS EXCITED. THE school's annual track and field meet was going to be held in Coaldale this year, which meant that I would be able to see Jenny again! It had been a whole year! She had exchanged letters with me for the first while, but then word from her had become less frequent, eventually stopping altogether. I thought her chores at home were probably keeping her busy.

As usual, I hadn't entered in any of the events, but the day of the meet I boarded the school bus heading out along with the other students. Bobby and Suzie had opted to stay home.

I was so excited. Soon I would be reunited with Jenny! I could hardly wait. We'd hang out and talk about old times. Maybe we would walk out to the fields where we used to play.

When we reached our destination, I felt a tinge of disappointment. I had never thought to question at which school the meet would be held. For some reason, I had just assumed it would be at my old school. Instead, it was being held at the public high. *Oh well, that's a minor thing.*

I looked about the grounds for Jenny, finally spotting her by the relay. She was just at the end of a race. I was a little surprised, since Jenny had never shown much interest in organized sports before.

I ran up to her. "Jenny!"

She turned around. "Korel!"

She seemed shocked to see me but not quite as ecstatic as I had hoped. But then, I figured, maybe that was just my imagination. I took a better look at her. Her hair was longer than it had been and it looked like it had been styled.

Before anything more could be said, a girl—a former classmate—came up to us. "Good going, Jenny!" Almost as an afterthought, she added, "Oh, hi, Korel."

Betty was popular—the type most other girls wanted to hang out with and be like. She had beautiful long black hair, had always worn pretty dresses to class, and was involved in school activities. Though Betty had never been snooty towards me—none of the girls really had—we hadn't associated much with each other.

"Hey, look. They're starting the broad jump," she now announced, beginning to run.

Jenny was close on her heels.

I couldn't recall Jenny being so friendly with Betty before. This reunion wasn't going quite as I had foreseen.

I trudged along behind.

BY THE END of the day, I realized it was over—part one of my life. My kinship with Jenny, the fun times, our races through the fields, and the side-by-side combat with a shared enemy, now lived only in the dimension called memory. It made me sad.

55

ONE LUNCH HOUR I sat in the gymnasium reconciled to the fact I would not be eating lunch that day. I had forgotten the usual boring sandwich on the counter at home.

Melanie, a girl I knew casually from my class, happened to see me sitting on the bench as she passed the open door.

"Where's your lunch?" she asked.

I explained.

"Why don't you come to my place for lunch?" she inquired. "I only live a couple of blocks from here."

I was surprised she would invite me since I didn't know her very well. I wasn't sure what to say. "Won't your mother mind?" I asked.

"No. Mom always makes lots at dinnertime."

I went with her and with trepidation followed Melanie into her kitchen. Her mother, Mrs. Chimco, made me feel welcome at once. "Come, sit and eat," she said, motioning me to a stool by the island table.

I spooned out a small ladleful of soup into the bowl placed in front of me.

"More, have more," Melanie's billowy Italian mother said, spooning extra soup into my bowl. "Eat. Eat. You have to eat more. You're so skinny."

Many people still considered me to be too thin. Though I had filled out some, I was still slender.

Before I left, Mrs. Chimco, with a heart as full as her figure, said, "Come for lunch every day."

So I did.

Mom and Joe offered to reimburse Mrs. Chimco, but she refused, saying, "I have to cook for my children everyday anyway. What's one more mouth?"

Melanie and I became good friends. She and I shared a common interest in animals and nature. We both took school seriously and had similar study habits. I didn't worry about appearing dim around her. Like me, she picked up a lot from reading. We spent time together discussing books we had read and helping each other with homework. Sometimes we would take a walk in the park. When winter eventually turned to spring, we'd sit and daydream on the lawn chairs in Melanie's backyard. Melanie wanted to go into conservation when she graduated.

"I want to be able to protect animals and their habitats," she said. "I want to make a difference."

I thought that was wonderful. I told her how I wanted to be a veterinarian. "Maybe we could even find jobs that would allow us to work together," I said.

On cold or rainy days we played board games in Melanie's room. Sometimes her brother, Mike, who was a year older, joined us.

Mike, like his Polish father, Mr. Chimco, was a gentle giant—at least in my eyes, since I was only four-foot-eleven at the time. Mike was a quiet, scholarly, soft-spoken guy who planned on taking commerce when he graduated.

One day in school, I noticed a few boys from Mike's class hazing him because of his height. "Hey, how's the weather up there?" they said. "Any magic beans up that pole?"

Mike just shrugged and grinned.

Now that I was older, I generally avoided confrontations, but Mike was my friend and no one was going to rib one of my friends. I defended him. "At least he's tall enough to find out. Not like you pipsqueaks!"

A few days later, the ringleader started in on Mike again.

"Leave him alone," I demanded. "Quit picking on him!"

For some reason, the bully found my anger enormously funny and began laughing and pointing at me.

His laughter fuelled my rage. I jumped up, slapped him, then grabbed Mike by the arm and steered him away from the boys.

I got a new nickname: "The Cat."

But Mike also came to my rescue once. It was in the fall while I was working in the garden. Joe had sent me out to pull up cornstalks. While I was out there, Mike and Melanie came to visit.

"What's your father thinking?" Mike said when he saw me. "You go sit on the bench and visit with Melanie. I'll do this." And he did. He pulled up and piled every stalk.

My two sets of friends—Melanie and Mike, and Suzie and Bobby—didn't associate much with each other. It wasn't that they disliked each other, they just had very little in common. Suzie and Bobby were much more action-oriented—they went bowling and to movies, they even auditioned for musicals; Suzie's dream was to one day star on Broadway—than Melanie and Mike.

But each pair gave me the best of both worlds.

56

MY HOUSE WAS on the very edge of town. Beyond the back fence lay open prairie. I was too old to play horse anymore, but every now and then the old spirit would take hold and I would toss my head, flare my nostrils and race Arnie down the field. Looking back, I think Arnie usually let me win.

Now that I lived in Lethbridge, I saw a lot more of Arnie and that suited me just fine. Arnie was about the only person in the whole world I could truly be myself with. He tolerated my idiosyncrasies and, upon reflection, he took a lot of guff from me. Like that day in early autumn...

We had decided to go hiking.

The day before, Suzie had made a batch of cookies. While preparing them, she sang along with the song on the radio, the one about the lifeguard. Only Suzie had changed the words:

Please don't talk to "Arnie."
Please don't talk to "Arnie."
Says the sign where I go to swim.
Oh-oh-oh-oh.
How can I get to know him?
How can I get to show him
that I am so much in love with him?
"Blond" and handsome, golden tan.
"Five-foot-five," man, oh, man!
Gotta make him mine, all mine.
Wish they'd take away that sign...

Arnie was Suzie's first crush. She had met him at my thirteenth birthday party and he had been on her mind ever since. She was always saying things like, "Arnie is so cute," or "Do you think Arnie would like this blouse?"

Now she was hoping to impress him with her homemade cookies. She suggested a hike and a picnic, and asked me to bring Arnie along.

We gathered at my place the next morning. Half a mile behind my house lay the coulees through which the Old Man River flowed. These semi-arid hills, home to cacti and rattlesnakes, offered adventure to Arnie, my friends and me. It was there we would hike today.

It was sunny as we set out on our trek, with just enough bite in the air to be wearing jeans and a sweater—an ideal day for a hike. The three of us trotted down the open prairie and twenty minutes later reached the edge of the ravine. Descending, we scuttled sideways, at times sliding on our butts, until we met the first fold in the land.

It was warm down in the gorge. Suzie and I removed our sweaters and Arnie took off his lightweight jacket. We paused for a moment. Here in the lee, more moisture accumulated and a few Saskatoon berry and chokecherry bushes had taken root in the sandy soil. Though the fruit of the former was finished for the season, the chokecherries would remain edible through late fall. I grabbed a handful, enjoying the sweet but astringent taste.

We followed the pass down to the next hill, gingerly avoiding prairie cacti. Ambling along, pausing here and there—Arnie found a snake's discarded rattle and put it in his pocket—we made our way down to the river. There, on soft green grass beneath the shade of a large poplar, we opened and passed around our brown bag lunch. Arnie had brought a thermos of Kool-Aid and I had made peanut butter and jam sandwiches.

Suzie waited until everyone had finished eating before opening her bag of cookies. "They're called chocolate kisses and here's one especially for you, Arnie."

Arnie brushed away her outreached hand. "I don't want your stupid kisses."

Suzie's face crumbled. I was furious with Arnie and refused to either look at or speak to him all the way back. When he phoned later that evening, asking for me, I refused to take his call. This continued for several days.

Arnie couldn't stand it when I refused to talk to him.

Finally, in desperation, he cornered me.

"All right already. I'm sorry. What do you want me to do?"

"Take her out to a show."

"No. No way. I don't want to take her anywhere."

Nose in the air, I walked away.

"All right. All right. I'll do it."

They went to see Blue Hawaii, *starring Elvis Presley.*

57

ON THE EAST end of the city two or three miles distant from where my house stood was a park. In the park was a man-made lake, Henderson Lake, where people could swim, though it has since been transformed into a Japanese garden. On hot, lazy summer afternoons, Arnie and I would walk there with my little blue transistor radio, listening to songs along the way like The Drifters' "Under the Boardwalk." That song fit those days perfectly.

Oh, when the sun beats down
and melts the tar upon the roof
and the sand gets so hot you wish
your tired feet were fireproof,
under the boardwalk,
down by the sea, yeah,
on a blanket with my baby
is where I'll be.

It was a long walk, but most of the streets in Lethbridge were tree-lined and we would scoot from elm to elm grabbing shade as we went along. Sometimes we'd hit it lucky and someone would have a sprinkler on that arced over onto the sidewalk.

Once at the lake, Arnie would jump right into the water and start swimming. Because I had never learned how to swim, I would instead try my luck at netting, with a sieve, one of the many goldfish that lived in Henderson Lake. It was said that pet owners who no longer wanted their fish released them there. I never did catch any but I had fun trying. Afterwards, Arnie and I would lounge about on the beach, eating the picnic lunch we had packed.

There was a nearby water tap we would use to fill the sealer jar we had brought with us. On one occasion while filling the jar, deserting our picnic bag in the process, a guy grabbed and ran off with the envelope of Kool-aid Arnie had packed. Spotting the culprit in the act, Arnie and I chased him down and made him return it.

The thief was indignant. "You that cheap? Like the commercial says, 'it only costs two cents a glass,'" he said.

"I don't care," I threw back at him. "It's ours."

IN THE WINTER, Henderson Lake was used as a rink. One frosty evening, the Grade 7 and 8 teachers set up a skating party there. My parents encouraged me to go. I didn't want to—I didn't know how to skate and had no interest in learning. Besides, none of my friends were going.

But Mom coaxed, "Go. You'll have fun, dear, you'll see. When I was young, I just loved skating."

Joe, in one of his "the world is a gala place" moods, agreed. He was happy that day so everyone else should be too. It didn't matter that he had given us grief the day before—that was the past. "Your Mom is right. You should socialize more, have fun."

I went, grudgingly.

A bonfire had been set up on the beach and hot chocolate was being served to the skaters as they came off the ice. I sat alone at the fire, watching one after another drift onto the ice.

You wouldn't catch me doing that. Prancing around like an idiot on knife blades.

A voice interrupted my thoughts. "I've got an extra pair of skates that just might fit you." It was Mr. Josten, the Grade 8 teacher.

"Oh. I, um, can't skate, but thank you anyway, Mr. Josten.

"Oh, come on—it's easy once you learn. Here, I'll help you put them on." He tugged them onto my feet, tightened the laces, and then called out to a boy in my class. "Frank. How about guiding this young lady around the pond?"

As Frank took me out, Mr. Josten said, "Don't worry. You're in good hands. You'll have a wonderful time."

No I would not! I didn't want to be out here skating. Everyone seemed to think they could just force me into feeling whatever they wanted me to feel—I say you're going to have fun and you're going to be happy whether you want to or not. That's all there is to it!

Oh, yeah? Well just try and make me! I'm sick and tired of everybody telling me what I should look like, think like, feel like!

"Um, I'm not very good at this," I said to the boy, stumbling.

"Ah, you're doing fine," he said, holding me upright.

How dare you say that! No, I am not *doing fine.*

He guided me out a little further. "See, it's not so bad, eh? Kind of fun, eh?"

"Oh yeah, I'm tickled pink," I replied sarcastically.

Frank seemed to find that amusing, which made me angrier yet.

We struggled along past other skaters, their faces aglow in the frosty air. "You know, you're actually doing pretty good," he said after a bit.

What! Next thing you know people will be leading me around like a bull with a ring in his nose, or putting a bat in my hand and telling me that I'm good at playing their beloved baseball, yet too.

I was definitely irate, but since Frank was being nice, I didn't want to offend him, so I glided along for a few more minutes. Against my will, I began finding the activity almost pleasurable. And that was the last straw!

"Thanks for teaching me, Frank, but, uh, my dad's supposed to be meeting me here in a few minutes, so if you don't mind, I should get back to shore."

"Oh, sure. I'll help you back to the fire."

Once ashore, I yanked off the offending skates and Frank went sailing back into the star-studded night.

There, I thought triumphantly. *I won!* But the glow I had anticipated didn't come.

"I don't want to be just another pebble in the gravel pit," I grumbled under my breath. "I want to be *me!*"

I felt melancholy and alone.

At the end of the evening when Joe came to pick me up, he asked if I had enjoyed myself.

"No. It was boring," I answered.

Joe looked disappointed.

When I got home, Mom asked in a hopeful voice, "Did you have a good time, dear?"

"No. I was bored."

Mom looked disappointed too.

That'll teach you guys.

58

I WOKE WITH A start. They were at it again. As far back as I could remember, I had been a light sleeper, like a well-trained German Shepherd, always on guard. I listened for a bit. The argument was escalating. I got up and peeked around the corner.

Joe, clad in a pair of white briefs, stood in the kitchen facing Mom, who was dressed in a pink filmy nightgown.

"You're cheating on me, I know it," he snarled.

"Maybe I should. Go find a man who'll treat me like a woman for a change and not like a dog," Mom threw at him.

"Neighbourhood slut. I'll cut you up so bad, no man will ever want you again." He went toward the cutlery drawer.

Mom grabbed the ring of keys off the wall and ran out the back door.

Barefoot, she scurried down the steps, across the walk and into the garage. Slamming the door behind her, she quickly locked it.

"Angelina," Joe called out. Ten seconds later, "Angelina. Get back in here!"

My mother heard the back door slam. She held her breath. There was silence.

Where was he? She shivered in the chilly autumn air.

The porch door creaked open. It shut.

Had he decided to leave her be? Not likely. Maybe he was throwing on some pants; he had been scantily dressed. Should she make a run for it?

She heard the door squeak open again.

He was at the garage. He rattled the doorknob. "Angelina, open this door!" *Thump. Thump, thump.* "Angelina!"

She looked about wildly. Where could she hide?

Again silence.

Why was he suddenly so quiet? The car portal! Just in time, she locked the latch.

"Look, Angelina," he said outside, "I just want to talk to you."

She held her tongue.

"I'm not going to hurt you." He paused. "For God's sake, quit being so dramatic, let me in!"

He waited, then trudged away, up the stairs and back into the house.

Why was he going back in, she wondered? And where was I? She knew it was unlikely I had slept through the disturbance. She opened the door a crack, in time to see him re-emerge with a tool kit.

"Oh, my God." She jumped in the car and locked the doors. The last time she had driven a vehicle was when she was fourteen—her dad's old Model T. But if need be...

"SIR, WHAT ARE you doing?"

Joe looked up to see two officers standing beside him.

He knew it was obvious that, screwdriver in hand, he was trying to jimmy the door. He gambled on honesty.

"I need to get into the garage, but the doors are locked and the keys are inside, so I'm trying to pry the door."

"Well, we received a complaint about a domestic disturbance. Is your wife here?"

"She's in the garage. We had a bit of a dispute, officer; it was a simple misunderstanding. My wife ran out into the garage, crying, and locked herself in. She is scantily dressed and I am worried that she might become hypothermic. You see, officer, my wife isn't mentally stable. She has been hospitalized in the past for attempted suicide. I've been trying to reason with her, convince her to come back into the house. She has the keys to the garage with her."

"Did you assault your wife?"

"No, sir. I did not. "

"Ma'am." The first officer knocked on the door. "This is the police. Are you in there?"

There was a muffled "Yes."

"Would you come out, please? We'd like to talk to you."

My mother emerged, draped in a wool blanket she had retrieved from the car.

The first officer gave her a brief once over: a good-looking, petite blonde, obviously shaken but bearing no visible bruises or other marks of physical assault.

"Did your husband hit you, ma'am?"

"No, sir."

"Why were you in the garage?"

"He said he was going to hurt me."

"Can you use his exact words?"

"I don't remember exactly what he said, but I knew he was going to stab me with a knife."

"Did he have a knife in his hand?"

"No, but he was running to get one."

"But you didn't see one in his hand?" The officer wrote in his notepad.

"No, sir. I ran away before he could get one," Mom said, shivering in the cool autumn air.

"Angelina, you're shaking, sweetheart." Joe tried to put his arm around her.

She edged away.

The officer spotted me standing in the doorway of the house, clothed in my pyjamas. "Is this your daughter?" he asked my mother.

Before Mom had a chance to reply, Joe confirmed it was, then quickly turned his attention back to my mother. "Now look, dear, what you've done. You've frightened Korel. Korel, go back to bed now. Everything will be all right. The officers will handle this. "

I stayed where I was. I wanted to speak up but knew that if I did, and they failed to believe me.... Joe could easily sway people. He could say something like my mother had brainwashed me, and then once the police had left there would be hell to pay.

"Sir," the officer said to Joe, "you have a nice wife and daughter here, but right now they're looking pretty shaken up. Try to tone it down in the future, all right?" He looked at Mom for a moment then back to Joe before adding, "I think maybe it would be best if you spent the night at a friend's. Just to let things cool down a bit."

The police escorted Joe to Uncle Jack's house. I was thankful. Uncle Jack had a calming way with Joe. My uncle wasn't brilliant like Joe was, he couldn't understand Einstein's theories, but over the years he had become Joe's best friend. On occasion, he and Arnie went camping with us. I liked it when they came along, because of Arnie most definitely, but also because of Uncle Jack. Uncle Jack seemed to know how to handle Joe and never tolerated any of his attitude. If Joe started in on Mom, Jack would simply tell him a soft but firm voice to shut up and Joe usually complied. Jack also insisted on hot dogs at the campsite rather than full course meals. And it was Uncle Jack who eventually convinced Joe to buy a freezer and a vacuum cleaner. Their relationship reminded me of an article I once read about temperamental racehorses. Sometimes trainers kept a placid pony in a stall next to the thoroughbred's because it pacified the more excitable animal. That's how Uncle Jack was—calm and steady.

By the time Joe returned home late the next morning, he had cooled down. Joe never suspected it was I, his fourteen-year old daughter, who had phoned the police. He was certain it had been the neighbours. We allowed him to continue thinking that.

59

JOE OFTEN SPOKE of the human brain and its abilities. He firmly believed that if a way could be discovered to properly harness it, the human brain would be capable of achieving great feats.

One day, gazing up at a star, I started reflecting upon his words. *What,* I wondered, *would happen if you hooked up your mind to the energy of a star?* I decided to try it. Sitting cross-legged on the grass, I focused on a star until I had reached a near hypnotic state, then, still gazing upward, I envisioned a student, Todd, who constantly bullied my friend Mike in school, falling down and hurting his leg.

The next morning, the bully was absent from school. The teacher informed us that Todd had wiped out on his motorbike and broken his leg.

Yes! It works!

A few days later, I came home to find my mother in tears. Joe had hit her again.

I decided that it was time for Joe to get his just rewards.

That evening I once again concentrated on the star, but this time I directed the combined energies towards Joe.

The following weekend—the Labour Day long weekend—we went camping for our last trip to the mountains for the year.

I no longer enjoyed going. For one thing, I was now a teen and found the whole camping scene boring. But there was another reason: I had come to fear Joe's driving. For the past few years, Joe had been employing various scare tactics and near misses. There were times when he was in one of his moods that he'd head toward a ditch or a tree and swerve away at the last possible second. Other times he would turn off the headlights while rounding hairpin mountain curves in the dark of night. If I begged him to stop, he'd taunt me by saying, "Why are you so afraid, Korel? Is it that you're so bad you fear you'll go to hell when you die?"

No, I wasn't afraid of death. It was the thought of the blood and the suffering, the carnage, and the thought of my mother writhing in agony.

But I need not have worried this time around. Joe was in a jovial frame of mind and was being exceptionally good to us during this trip. I had even been permitted to bring Arnie along.

We were on our way back home when the weather turned nasty. We were hit by a fall storm that turned quickly from rain to snow.

"I'm driving slower than usual tonight," Joe said. "I want to make sure I get all of you, my extra special cargo, home safely."

We were near Fort McLeod, about an hour's drive from home, when I dozed off—something I normally didn't allow myself to do in a moving vehicle. I was startled awake by Joe's frantic shout, "Oh, my God, brace yourselves, we're going to crash!"

I heard the screeching of tires and simultaneously saw the car in front of us. Then came the smashing sound of breaking headlights, the slow grind of metal, followed by the shattering of glass as the windshield cracked.

Then silence.

I felt calm. I tried my door. It was jammed. I spotted Mom in the front, lying on the floor, motionless. In the back of the wagon, Arnie also lay still. I heard moaning from the driver's seat and in the dim moonlight saw Joe—blood pouring down his face and covering his hands—reach out for me.

Panic set in. I began screaming and frantically pounding on my window. A bright light appeared out of nowhere and shone in my face.

The light had a voice. "It's all right, little girl. Everything will be okay. I'll get you out."

The door was pried open. I jumped out and began racing in circles, barefoot, through a puddle of rain and melting snow.

"Miss, come sit in my car," a police officer said.

I ran. I couldn't stop. Around and around I went, faster and faster.

Then flashing lights. Flashing, swirling blood lights. Wails of the denizens of hell. Reflections of blood-red and of tortured souls leaping off the wet pavement.

"Korel, Korel."

Mom?

"It's okay, dear. We're all going to be okay."

I wanted to go to her but my legs wouldn't stop moving in their relentless orbit. Then the bloody, screaming outrider of doom fled the scene with Joe. Quiet ensued.

Exhausted, I sank down into my puddle and allowed the officer to escort me to his car.

I took in the scene. We had hit the back of a car parked on the shoulder of the road. Joe was on his way to the hospital, but the officer wanted to get our statement before taking the rest of us there.

"What did you see?" the patrolman questioned me.

"A car suddenly in front of us."

"Did it have its lights on?"

"No, officer, it didn't."

"Are you certain about that? Could you be mistaken?" He kept asking me the same questions over and over again.

Finally, I—uncharacteristically, with adults at least—lost my temper. "Look, officer. I saw what I saw."

When we arrived at the hospital, it was discovered that Joe was being treated for broken ribs and lacerations, that Mom had a dislocated shoulder and that Arnie, who had been knocked out, had a mild concussion. My only injury was a small blood blister on one of my fingers. Apparently none of the occupants of the car we hit were injured.

We learned later that the driver of the car we had hit was a cop's son. The officer had pulled him over on the highway for an undisclosed reason and had turned off the cruiser's revolving lights. Joe insisted when later questioned in court that the parked car had no lights of any sort on either. Furthermore, he said, it was parked overlapping the driving lane. Mom, Arnie and I were again questioned and our story coincided with Joe's. Nonetheless he was found to be at fault.

But I knew who was really at fault. Me. I was the one who had flung the dark energy at Joe. As a result, he, along with innocent others, had suffered. And not only had I dabbled in things I had no business dabbling in, I had also let my guard down. I had dozed off while he had been driving. I now knew that someday, sooner or later, I would have to pay the consequences—likely when I least expected it.

My nervousness in cars became a phobia.

60

MY MOTHER OPENED a business. It was after one of Joe's shoving and slapping tirades, when he "owed her one." She rented a suite on the main floor of an apartment building close to the downtown area and set up a clinic.

The skill of bone-setting had been handed down along the maternal side of Mom's family for generations. Her education had been furthered in that area through a course she had taken in physiotherapy in Detroit, while living in the Windsor area. And from her Grandmother Bickert on her father's side, she had received at an early age an understanding of local herbs growing on the prairies and their healing properties. Later, on her frequent forays to the Rockies, she had familiarized herself with medicinal plants found there as well. She read material on herbs from other countries. Now, combining her skills and knowledge and the experience she had obtained from working in various medical institutions, she set up an herbal massage clinic.

The clinic offered treatment for a variety of ailments from dislocated bones to psoriasis. Word spread quickly and before long people looking for alternative healing began arriving at her door, in spite of the fact that some doctors called her a quack.

After a couple of months, Joe tried to renege on his agreement with my mother, complaining that her clinic took up too much of her time, but on this matter she stood her ground.

"I will not give up my clinic. If you try to stop me, I'll leave you for good and I will tell everyone, all your friends, everybody, what you do to me."

He was left with no alternative but to honour his word.

Patients from out of town needing lengthy treatments stayed in her clinic in the overnight room, which could accommodate two people. Mom hired me, on an after-school basis, to wash their dishes, change their bedding, and to help clean and tidy the rest of the clinic as well.

I was learning bookkeeping and filing in school and found I had a knack for it. I discovered that there was something very satisfying about making figures balance and putting accounts in their proper places. So Mom decided to employ me to look after that end of her business also.

61

"KOREL, I'M GOING away for a couple of days," my mother was saying. "I'm going to Calgary, but tell your dad you know nothing, that I never told you where I was going."

"You're going to see *him,* aren't you?"

Him was a reflexologist, a person who works on people through their feet, with a healing business of his own in Calgary. Passing through Lethbridge one day, Larry had seen Mom's sign: *A's Herbal Therapeutic Massage Centre.* Curious, he had walked in. Larry had been very impressed with my mother's work, and now, whenever he was in Lethbridge—which seemed to be more and more frequently—he stopped in at the clinic. I didn't mind him at first, he was just another guy, but before long it became obvious that he was interested in more than my mother's clinic.

"I don't like him," I had told her, "I don't like the way he looks at you."

She had made light of it, insisting they were just friends.

"Yes, I am going to see Larry," Mom now admitted, "but it's for business reasons only. I want to go and see his healing centre."

It sounded like a plausible excuse, but I just had this feeling that it was more than that. I wished he would stay away from my mother. There was going to be trouble. What was I supposed to tell Joe? He was sure to be mad because she had left without having an "excuse"—they hadn't fought lately.

I wished Mom and I could just leave Joe once and for all, but without getting another man involved.

I hated the times I had to be alone with my father. I hated having to sit there listening to him rattle on about how horrible Mom was. And I didn't like the way he would be so nice to me, in that sickly, syrupy way of his. It made me nervous and uncomfortable, as if I was walking on a tightrope.

I never told Mom any of this, however. I merely said he was good to me whenever we were alone. My job, as I saw it, was to preserve peace in the home. Besides what really could I say—that he was *too* nice to me?

WHEN I GOT home from school, I set to work cleaning the house. It wouldn't stop Joe from raving but it would help appease the situation a little. Joe was a believer in hard work. There was no sleeping in on weekends at our house. One should be up and about doing something.

I now scurried about, running from room to room, doing, as Mom called it, *"from bowen awa,"* which, in *Plautdietsch* means, *on top of,* or *up over.* Cleaning the obvious. A little of this and a little of that: the dishes, a quick swipe of the floor, tossing scattered books and magazines under the sofa and throwing together the bed.

Mom and I had a habit of letting things go, of letting the dust and dishes pile up, and then, when Joe got angry, or during one of her cleaning spurts, she and I would spend days cleaning thoroughly.

How was I to cover for Mom? I worried as I worked. *Let's see, Grosma or Bopa is sick?* No, he'd phone and realize that was a lie. But to say Mom hadn't told me where she was going? I must prepare myself mentally for he was sure to rant about that.

And he did. "What kind of mother is that who would just up and leave without saying where she's going? What if something happened to you and I couldn't get hold of her?"

She's done it before, when you knew you were to blame. You didn't mind then.

"I'm sure it must have been important, Daddy. She wouldn't leave without a good reason."

"Have you seen any men about lately? I mean, do men come to her clinic?"

"Well, there is an old man that comes. He's in a wheelchair and has to use a diaper, and there's another man who has psoriasis all over his face and hands."

"Oh," he replied, no longer interested.

In truth, it was an old woman in the wheelchair and a young woman with the psoriasis. There was also middle-aged Larry.

"Well, the hell with her. At least *you're* still here. Let's go out and have a burger and chips."

When we got back home, Joe started on a bottle of wine. He drank a few glasses, then said, "How about having a drink with your old man?"

He poured me a drink. *"Nazdrowie,"* he said, clinking his glass with mine.

This wasn't the first drink we'd had together. He'd been slipping me drinks since I was thirteen, over a year ago. I didn't much care for wine so I sipped very slowly, dumping my glass whenever I got the chance.

"Why can't your mother be more like you? You I can talk to. You and I, we understand each other. We get along just fine. Come on, drink up, drink up."

I dipped my lip in the glass. Where were his drinking buddies when I needed one?

"Why can't your mother love me? She's a witch, you know. She's so beautiful that she casts spells on men, makes them fall for her." He was getting drunk.

"But you, you're not like that, you're a good girl. You're my best friend. You know that? You, I can trust."

Shut up. Quit talking so nice to me!

"You would never stab me in the back."

Gutless, two-faced hypocrite, that's what I am. Why can't I just look him in the eye and tell him the truth about how I really feel about him?

Because you don't want to hurt him, that's why.

Why shouldn't I want to hurt him? He's hurt Mom and me plenty.

I didn't want to hear any more of it—not his biting words about Mom, nor his sugary praises of me. How much longer before he got tired and went to bed?

I WOKE TO a presence in my room. It was my father. I feigned sleep. He bent over me, kissed my forehead, paused, then crawled into my bed.

THE NEXT MORNING, Joe said, "About last night. I'm sorry. I just didn't want to be alone. You—you understand, don't you? I didn't really do anything wrong. I mean, it's not as though I hurt you in any manner. You know I would never do that. Let's just keep this between you and me, okay?"

I felt dirty and that horrid presence in the pit of my stomach was back—that wretched, lonely, sad...*thing*.

"BUT KOREL KNEW where I was, I told her I was going to visit my sister Rose in Calgary," Mom asserted.

Joe had reproached her for leaving without telling him where she was going.

I felt the sting of deep hurt—all that I had put up with just so Mom could get away! Not once had I let on that I knew what she was up to. I had protected her, and this was the thanks I got? Betrayal?

He's right after all. She doesn't really love me.

I confronted my mother at the first opportunity. "Why did you do that to me, Mom? Why did you tell him I knew where you were?"

"I...I wasn't thinking. I don't know what made me say that. I'm so sorry." She reached out to me. "You know I love you, don't you? That I'd never do anything to hurt you on purpose? Please, Korel, say you'll forgive me." Tears rolled down her cheeks.

I couldn't do it. I just couldn't stay mad at her. I told her I forgave her. And I truly did try to understand, but I was too hurt to let her hug me.

62

CHRISTMAS WAS JUST a little over a week away. The spruce was set up in its usual place by the living room window. Joe wound the lights up and around the tree, making the whole procedure look easy. By the time he was done, there were no empty branches, and no two bulbs of the same colour side by side.

Christmas was special to Joe. It was a time for the exchange of gifts, good food, laughter, and play. There had always been fighting and arguing on that day when he was a child. He had vowed that it wouldn't be like that when he had his own family. True to his word, he never lost his temper on Christmas Day.

I hung a glass icicle on the tree. While only Joe strung the lights, Mom and I helped with the rest of the decorating.

The Christmas season was usually a wonderful, happy time for me, though I had never quite been able to capture the beauty and awe of that one special day, years ago, when I had been so sick. But then, I reasoned, perhaps such magic occurred only at death's door.

One thing I didn't like about Christmas, though, was the pre-cleaning. My mother was quite adamant that the celebration, particularly the New Year's part of it, could not be held in a dirty house. "However it is on New Year's Eve," she'd say, "so will it be the rest of the year." Therefore each room had to be given a thorough going over—no *from bowen awa*. "Forget about the dishes. Ignore the laundry. It's *cleaning* time."

I hated it. I didn't like the week-long chaos, the mess that major cleaning created, or the dust that made me sneeze and itch. Fortunately that part of Christmas was almost finished for the year.

On the morning of Christmas Eve, Mom, with my help, would begin preparing the main dishes. She would make the *warenekje*—perogies—by rolling a fistful of the dough at a time, then cutting out circles with a drinking glass. Each disk would then receive a filling and be folded over, with the edges pinched together to insure that it all stayed intact when boiled the next day. Fillings from both cultures were used: Mennonite *glums*—cottage cheese, onion, and beaten egg yolk; the Polish diced *kielbasa* and sauerkraut; prune; potato and cheese.

Mom used only the small inner leaves of cabbage to make her dainty cabbage rolls, which she filled with a mixture of beef and pork hamburger, cooked rice and barley, onions and various spices.

One of Joe's favourite dishes, *Kielbasa Kapus'ciany*—which consisted of sauerkraut, chopped cabbage, sausage and plenty of paprika—would need to be sautéed on low heat for a number of hours. The *schmuadenett*, a Mennonite delicacy made from pork-hock jelly and lemon-flavoured gelatin, would have already been made the day before and put outside. Since we didn't have enough room in the fridge, and didn't yet own a freezer, a few of the dishes had to be placed in a box in the garage so they could be kept cold.

Just before going to bed, Mom would stuff the turkey with *baubut*—a mixture of breadcrumbs, flour, turkey giblets, fruit and spices—and bake it overnight in a slow oven at 275 degrees F. Christmas morning, the turkey would be so tender you could cut the meat with a butter knife.

Christmas Day in our home always began just before sunrise with Joe and I, still dressed in our pyjamas, and Mom in her prettiest nightgown and housecoat, gathering in the living room. Joe would take his place by the tree and hand out the presents, slowly, one at a time, savouring each opening. We always unwrapped the gifts carefully because Mom liked to reuse the paper.

She could combine leftover scraps from previous years and yet make her gifts look like a professional had wrapped them. She had taken a brief course on giftwrapping at a department store where she once worked in Ontario. Joe too was a fair hand at wrapping. But the outside of my presents looked decidedly amateurish. I didn't enjoy wrapping presents. I found it to be a slow, painful process. First you had to measure the item and then the paper. Next you had had to try to cut straight and then somehow centre the gift in the paper. Mine refused to do that; there was always too little or too much on each end. I would begin to yawn and hyperventilate, feeling as though I wasn't getting enough air as I forced myself to slow down and try to get it right. The next step, the folding, was almost as bad. If you were lucky, you had an end that you then taped down. But most of the time my end was pointy, like a thick, fat tail. I was always glad when that part of Christmas prep was over.

After the opening, most of the gifts would be put back under the tree for a day or so, so the spot wouldn't suddenly look so bare.

Then we would have a light breakfast of fruit and cereal. We would begin working on Christmas dinner around eleven o'clock. While most of the dishes had only to be heated in the oven or on the stove, there were the mashed potatoes to be prepared and perogies to be boiled.

My mother would have preferred a dining room as she'd had in Coaldale in which to serve the feast, but the kitchen table had to suffice. It would be covered with the cranberry-coloured cloth, which would remain there for the duration of the festive season. Mom would have liked to cover the cloth with clear plastic to make it easier to clean, but Joe wouldn't hear of it.

"That is the lazy woman's way of doing things," he contended.

The table was set with Mom's finest china. The teapot and two of the serving bowls had been handed down to her from her maternal grandmother.

The meal would usually be ready by around one o'clock. Arnie and Uncle Jack would often join us. Of course, this made the day extra special for me.

Once the table was cleared—"Never mind the dishes, today is Christmas," Joe would say—the Monopoly game would be set up, with Joe acting as banker. Amidst cracking nuts, gulping pop, and nibbling on dainties—"Christmas Day is for eating," Joe always insisted—we would travel up and down the board, stained by Christmases past, with our horse or thimble or wheelbarrow as Bing Crosby and other vocalists entertained us with carols.

I'm dreaming of a white Christmas,
just like the ones I used to know,
where the treetops glisten
and children listen
to hear sleighbells in the snow.

The next day, Boxing Day, the festivities would continue with reheated leftovers.

YES, THE CHRISTMAS season was usually a special time for me, but this year I was confused. Heavy things weighed on my mind. Two weeks had passed since the weekend I had been alone with my father, and I had yet to tell my mother what he had done.

Mom and I usually kept very little from each other, but I wasn't sure how I should handle this. It wasn't in me to "squeal" and I liked to handle my own problems. I didn't like the thought of people thinking of me as a helpless maiden in distress, searching for sympathy. Neither was I an instigator. I wanted peace in my home, not more conflict, and I knew this could most certainly flare up into a fight between Mom and Joe. Mom allowed Joe to slap her around but tended to draw the line when it came to me.

And there were extenuating circumstances to consider. He *had* been drunk, and he *had* apologized the next day.

I know, but what he did was wrong. It was gross and disgusting, I argued.

But it wasn't rape; he didn't actually harm me.

"My little girl. The one person I can trust."

His words played over and over in my head. Would telling be a betrayal of that trust, a back-stabbing?

63

After much debate, I had finally decided what to do about my problem. The bottom line was that I just didn't want to be left alone with Joe anymore; his hugs made me feel like worms were crawling all over me. I would simply tell Mom I didn't want her to leave anymore.

With feelings of trepidation I approached Mom the next morning. *How to say it?*

"Mom, please don't leave me alone next time you go away somewhere."

"But I don't, Korel. Your dad is here."

Oh boy! She's complicating it. "Yeah, I know—but..."

My mother went still. She knew; she didn't know how she knew but she knew. Still she had to ask. "Did something happen, Korel?"

"He touched me. You know," I stammered, red-faced.

"You mean there?"

I nodded.

"Did he...?"

"No." I cut my mother's words short. I knew what she was about to ask. "But this wasn't the first time either."

"What!" Mom's face went white.

What have I just said?

I realized my words were true. My mouth had remembered something my mind had forgotten. This *wasn't* the first time. He had come to my bed before, when Mom was in hospital after her attempted suicide. How could I have forgotten? I remembered the waves of nausea, that familiar feeling of utter loneliness and despair.

A cold calm born of inner rage washed over Mom.

"Korel, I want you to go to Melanie's house after school. Don't come home until I call you."

"Mom, what are you planning on doing?" I asked, suddenly afraid. "Mom, don't tell him I told you, please. He—he didn't actually do 'it' to me. He didn't hurt me. I—I just don't want you to leave me alone with him anymore, that's all."

"Korel, do what I say," my mother said sternly.

MOM TOLD ME about it afterwards. She had been waiting for him when he came home after work.

"What did you do to Korel?" she exploded.

Joe had never seen her look at him like that before, like he was some kind of lowly insect. He shivered. "What do you mean?"

"You know damn well what I mean. For twenty-two years I've put up with your bullshit, your beatings. It was always, "Yes, Joe; no, Joe," but what you did to Korel—that's the last straw. Pack your things and get out of here," she screamed, advancing toward him.

He lifted his fist.

"Don't you dare," she hissed, "or so help me God I'll kill you. I'll find a way."

"I—I didn't hurt her," he stammered. "I wouldn't do that. She's still pure."

"Get out!" Mom advanced towards him, hatred in her eyes.

He knew she had reached her limit. He scurried out.

SHE MADE THE call. I picked up. "It's over, Korel. You can come home now."

"It was so simple," Mom said later. "I just told him to get out. To think of all those years we suffered. 'Yes, Joe. No, Joe.' It makes me sick. Why did I do that? You and I could have had a good life together instead of living in fear. Maybe if I had just stood up to him like I did today, he might even have turned out to be a good husband. Well, whatever, thank God it's finally over."

I, however, had my doubts. Maybe I was being a pessimist but I couldn't see it being this easy, and said as much to Mom.

"No. I've got him over the barrel now," she replied. "There'll be no more trouble."

THE NEXT DAY at school, I was called to the classroom door. Joe was standing there. He would be taking me out for the remainder of the afternoon, he told the teacher. I knew I was in for it. His eyes were deep caverns, his breath slow and steady so as to keep his emotions in check.

Some might ask, "Why didn't you refuse to go with him?" or "Why didn't you ask for help from the teachers?" Well, it wasn't in me to ask for help, and even if I had, what would I have said—that he's fit to kill? They wouldn't have understood or, likely, even believed me. A well-spoken, well-dressed man like Mr. Jaslo, who had a steady job, would never beat his family. That kind of thing only happened among Indians or the poor. And if Mr. Jaslo did spank his child on occasion, well, surely she must deserve it, mustn't she?

I felt like an animal headed for the slaughterhouse. Joe didn't utter a word during the drive home and I knew better than to speak. Instead, I tried to prepare myself for the inevitable, whatever that might be.

What if he's killed Mom? No. Mom would still be at work. But what if he's brought her home? What if she's lying in a pool of blood? What is he planning on doing to me? Whatever, I must not cry. No matter what I see or what happens, I must be strong.

When we walked into the house, my father confronted me. "Because of you, your mother is leaving me." He forced me over a chair. He removed his belt. "It's all your fault."

Shwap. Shwap.

I feel nothing.

"I thought you were a good girl."

Shwap. Shwap.

I am strong.

"I trusted you." His voice held a quaver.

He dropped the belt, turned to stand in front of me. "Korel, look at me." Tears were pouring down his cheeks. "I loved you, I trusted you, and you betrayed me, Korel."

His words stung worse than the strap.

Don't listen to him, Korel. Happy. Happy. Happy Korel.

"How is it that you can be so cold, so...so *unfeeling,* so reptilian? I never raised you this way." Joe's words were anguished. He looked into my eyes and horror began to flood his own. "You...you're not—not human, are you?" he stammered.

Happy Korel. Happy, happy Korel.

He began backing away. "God help me, I've raised the devil!"

Joe stumbled out the door, threw himself into the car and sped away as though he spied the gates of hell opening beneath him.

64

I WATCHED HIM DRIVE away. *What should I do? Get away from here before he comes back.*

I ran the two blocks to the bus stop, making it just in time before the bus left.

Choosing a seat in the back, I sat down. In the safety of the city transit I began to shake. I shook so badly my teeth started chattering. I couldn't stop. *Thank goodness there's no one sitting near me to witness this.*

An image of Joe's terrified face came up on my mental screen. What had happened back there? *There must be something about me that he can see and I can't, some power he is afraid of.*

A thrill rippled through me. I was more powerful than he was. I had won!

Fury reigns triumphant!

We were free; Mom and I were free at last.

But... "You betrayed me, Korel," his words repeated in my head.

Shut up! I'm not going to let you spoil my victory. I'm happy! I'm happy!

I smiled. And in a state of elation, I floated off the bus and into my mother's clinic.

Mom was working on a patient. The woman, in her fifties, was lying face down on a massage table with towels—soaked in a mixture of apple cider vinegar, Epson salts, Hammer's soda, salt and various herbs—on her neck and upper back. My mother slowly swung an infrared lamp back and forth over the rags.

I was still shaky. I hoped my mother would notice. Not, of course, that I wanted or needed any sympathy, but I wouldn't have minded a little admiration for my bravery and victory over our mutual enemy.

"How was school today, dear?"

"Fine." I wasn't about to tell her otherwise in front of a patient, even if she was a regular.

Mom switched off the lamp, hung it on its stand, and removed the towels from Mrs. Davis's back and neck. She reset the timer, then—with small but strong hands—began the massage, kneading the patient's stiff muscles.

By the time my mother had finished and Mrs. Davis was resting with a cup of camomile tea in hand, my shaking had ceased. I was almost tempted to try to re-establish the tremors, but that would be so phoney, quaking just to get my Mom's attention. No, the moment had passed.

"Well, Mom, we really are free now."

"Yes. Praise the Lord."

"I saw him today, you know," I threw out tentatively.

"You did? Where?"

"At school. He came and brought me home. He gave me a lickin' for tattling on him." I felt like a cowardly informer for "tattling" about this yet now too.

Mom gasped. "He brought you home and spanked you for telling me? That asshole of a man! He isn't even a man."

"After he gave me the lickin', he got this scared look on his face and ran out."

"Guilt. Probably guilt for what he did."

"I don't think so."

"Maybe God intervened, then."

"Maybe."

I wanted to say, "He knows I am powerful," but I knew that you must never blow your own horn, for if you did, you might lose whatever it was you were bragging about.

"I think, Korel, we should spend the night here, not go home. There are no overnight patients tonight."

I didn't comment. Though I wasn't eager to go back to the house either, I was afraid that agreeing would make me appear cowardly.

Joe phoned the clinic that evening, pleading with Mom, asking her to just see him, talk to him. She insisted she didn't want anything more to do with him, and when he phoned the second time, she hung up, leaving the phone off the hook.

Later, when we were getting ready for bed, we could have sworn we heard someone trying the outside door, and that we saw a man's shadow behind the waiting room window's blinds.

I had to use the toilet during the night. The bathroom was bathed in the muted glow of the outside street lamp, so I left the door ajar and the light off. When I was done and washing my hands, I caught a glance of myself in the mirror. The words "I've raised the devil," sounded in my head. Afraid of what I might see in my reflection, I tore my eyes away and rushed back to bed, pulling the covers over my head.

We had a fitful night and the next morning, tired, we slept late. Mom didn't open to the public and I stayed home from school. We agreed that since the apartment building was a more public place, it was probably safer than the house. Joe might be afraid of me, I reasoned, but I didn't plan on pushing my luck. If power was used recklessly or flaunted, it might be taken away.

We made plans. Since Joe wasn't going to leave us, we would leave him. We would go home just long enough to pack boxes and a suitcase each, then take a cab back here with the luggage. Until we found a place of our own, we would live in the clinic.

Before we could leave for the house, however, a woman with a dislocated shoulder came to the clinic door. My mother didn't have the heart to turn her away. By the time we managed to get on the city bus, it was three in the afternoon.

Though Joe was likely at work, we took no chances. After all, he had taken off work yesterday afternoon just to retrieve me from school. We approached the house from the rear by first crossing into the neighbour's backyard. I stealthily edged forward, motioning Mom to stay put. It had snowed late last night, and there were footprints from the house to the garage but no prints leading back. There were fresh tire tracks in the driveway. I signalled the okay.

The packing progressed slowly, too slowly for my liking. My mother was not known for haste. Whatever she tackled was done well but in due time; there was never any sweeping of crumbs under the rug with her. "Do it right or not at all," which is why she often neglected her housework. Today was no different. She took her time, carefully folding each item before placing it in a box or in her suitcase, and tried to encourage me to do the same. "Oh, we should grab this," she said, "and we need that."

The phone began ringing off and on. After an hour of trying to ignore it, Mom lifted the receiver. It was Joe. He was drunk. "I've got a gun and I'm going to kill you and Korel."

My mother dropped the menacing harbinger of evil. Blood rushed to her head. What should she do? Phone the police? By the time they showed up, she and I could be dead. Was it just an idle threat? She gingerly picked up the dangling receiver, listening. There was silence on the other end. He had hung up.

When faced with an emergency, Mom was usually able to think quickly. She phoned a taxi and arranged to meet it at the corner of the street, down a block. We grabbed one suitcase each, and slipped out through the back and into the field beyond.

We trudged forward, stumbling in the dark through calf-deep snow, struggling with the extra weight of our luggage. Snow filled our boots but adrenaline kept us from feeling the cold. Would Joe catch us before we could make it to the corner?

Panting, Mom and I neared the point of rendezvous. We avoided the streetlight and stood concealed in the shadow of a tree. Time ticked slowly as we waited anxiously for the cab. Would we make our escape?

Then we saw it coming down the street. Mom and I dashed forward and jumped in.

65

"TO THE KETHBRIDGE HOTEL," Mom instructed the driver. "And please hurry."

The cabby put his foot to the floor.

Not more than two minutes later, we spotted Joe's car. He drove right past the cab, not noticing us.

When we reached the hotel, my mother booked a room under a fictitious name.

What to do now? we wondered.

"I'll phone Larry," Mom decided.

My mother and the reflexologist had struck up a friendship that over time had developed into something deeper. Larry wasn't much to look at, she knew, and he was nearly blind, but he treated her with respect.

She hadn't yet told me—she knew I didn't care much for Larry—that he had tried to talk her into moving, along with me, to his apartment in Calgary. "You and I could combine our skills and open a large healing centre. I'm well-to-do. You and Korel would not be left wanting," he had said.

But Mom had hesitated. "Korel has friends here," she said, "and I don't want to give up my clinic."

Then, a couple of weeks ago, days after Mom had gone to see him in Calgary, Larry had temporarily closed his business and moved into a suite in the same apartment building as Mom's clinic.

"Larry," Mom now said on the payphone. "Korel and I are running away from Joe. He's threatened to kill us."

Larry said he'd be right down.

When Larry showed up at our hotel room, he asked if we had called the police.

"No," Mom answered.

"Well, call them and tell them he's threatened you."

"No, Larry. I've tried that before, it doesn't work. He's smart. He knows how to talk himself out of tight corners. He'll just end up making me look like the fool or the crazy one."

I came to a sudden realization. *There are many types of power. Joe's power is the power of speech—the ability to get people to believe what he's saying, like a politician or a lawyer.* This was something I had known all my life but not been able to put into words. *How is it possible to know something but not know something? I'm going to have to give this some thought.*

"You and Korel can come with me to Calgary. You'll be safe there."

"No. You don't realize just how dangerous he can be. I won't have you hurt because of me."

"But, Angelina..."

"No." Mom set her jaw. She could be quite stubborn at

times. "Please, Larry. We're going to take the bus to Saskatoon in the morning. I'll phone you when we get there."

"What will the two of you do once you get there?"

"We'll go to my mom and dad's."

"But you've said that your mother just talks you into returning every time."

"This time it will be different. There isn't just me to consider, there's Korel too."

"Will the two of you be safe there?"

"As long as I don't let him talk me into going anywhere alone with him, I'll be all right. He wouldn't dare try anything in front of my dad. He's scared of him."

"Oh, Angelina. Won't you please reconsider?"

Larry's father had warned him. "Son, she's one of those women who will never really leave her husband," he had said. "Oh, sure, maybe she'll leave him for a while, but eventually she'll go back. Best forget her." But Larry couldn't. He loved her too much.

Before he left, he reached into his pocket and pulled out a hundred dollars. "Here," he said to Mom. "Take it. And phone, okay?"

THE NEXT MORNING, Mom and I took a cab out to the bus depot and purchased tickets to Saskatoon. Boarding the coach, we found an empty double seat near the middle. I chose the side by the window.

The bus had barely left the terminal when Mom began talking to a passenger across the aisle, a woman with large lesions on her face.

"Oh, you poor dear," my mother sympathized, "I have a herbal clinic. I could help you. I've cured others of psoriasis before. Remember Irma, Korel?" Mom asked, looking at me, "how bad a case she had?"

I'm not her daughter.

Red-faced, I slid down in my seat, hoping I'd find a space to crawl into. Sometimes Mom could be so embarrassing. It seemed she had never learned the rule: don't point out the fat lady.

Still, there were times I envied her openness and spontaneity with people. For though this trait of hers offended some people, many others, after getting over the initial shock and sensing that her concern was genuine, opened up to her.

By contrast, every word that came out of my own mouth was weighed and measured; every move I made calculated, so that I would appear mature and intelligent. No adult that I knew of, other than that Grade 6 teacher and Joe, suspected I might be a dimwit.

Though I was sure that my peers in school knew. I wasn't witty nor did I know how to flirt like other girls did. And I couldn't crack a joke. Half the time when others jested, I didn't even get the punchline, though I pretended to. Sometimes it was even I who was the brunt of their jokes. Like the time a few girls in class complimented me on my apparel—an emerald-green nylon blouse and a crimson wool skirt. "Nice outfit," they had said.

"Thank you," I had replied, beaming. I had rather liked the combo myself, thinking it looked kind of Christmas-y.

It wasn't until they were out of earshot that Suzie informed me that what I had taken as a compliment was actually sarcasm.

At times I wondered how it was that my four friends, especially Suzie and Bobby, who were so outgoing, liked me.

I looked out the window; we had just pulled out of Taber, the small southern Alberta town known for its sugar beets and sweet corn. I could see snow beginning to fall.

In Medicine Hat, where we changed buses, we grabbed a quick lunch during the half-hour layover.

At each stop we prepared ourselves mentally, half expecting to see Joe waiting for us. We agreed that we would be glad once we reached Saskatoon. But then again we worried that, anticipating our move, he might very well show up at the depot there. We would have to be vigilant.

The wind picked up and the snow began to fall more heavily. Traffic slowed to a crawl. The bus pulled into Swift Current forty-five minutes late. We were informed that due to the snowstorm the buses would not be running any further that night. A man and woman, at the depot to meet their daughter, took pity on us and gave us a lift to a nearby hotel. But due to the snowstorm and the fact that Christmas was only two days away, there were no available rooms, not there nor at any of the other hotels.

Desperate, Mom made a reverse call to her baby brother, Ike. Though Ike was the youngest of the family of eight, there was nothing "baby" about him. Built short but tough, there was little in life that daunted him. He said the weather wasn't all that bad on his end and that he'd come and get us. Weary, we waited in the lobby of the hotel.

It took Ike and his friend Pete three and half-hours to make the one-hundred-and-sixty-five-mile drive from Saskatoon to Swift Current. Then, after coffee and a bite to eat, they were ready to once again battle the storm.

"Well, sis," Ike said to my mother in the car. "You decided to leave the bastard. I hope it's for good this time."

"Oh, yes. You better believe it is!" Mom said adamantly. This time he went too far. He—"

Fearful of how much she planned on saying, I nudged her and gave her a grimace.

She returned my look and gave me a barely perceptible

shake of her head. "He threatened us with a gun. He said he was going to shoot us. Korel and I barely escaped with our lives."

"If you had left years earlier, Korel wouldn't have had to go through all that."

"I know," my mom sighed.

"Why'd you put up with his bullshit for so long?"

"I don't know. Because I'm stupid, I guess."

"What kind of answer is that?"

"Well, it's true."

"Your problem is that you just put up with too much shit. You don't have a backbone. You should have put him in line years ago."

"Well, I gave him what-for the other day for..." Mom glanced at me, "for something he did and now look what's happened," she retorted.

"You should have let me put a lickin' on him that time I wanted to. Like I told you before, he's a coward."

Her brother wasn't saying anything she hadn't thought before. It was true, she reflected. Joe never raised his voice when Ike was around, nor did he make any demands on her. One scowl from Ike and Joe would quickly back down. But after Ike left, she was the one who would suffer for it.

WHILE THE OTHERS talked, I sat huddled in the backseat near the door, trembling in true earnest. My car phobia was acting up. *Maybe today is pay-day.* I felt helpless and confined, at the mercy of the driver.

I stared fixedly out the window ahead. I must remain attentive. Uncle Ike was too busy giving Mom what-for to notice that there was a full-fledged prairie blizzard blowing out there. It was impossible to see more than a few feet ahead.

Mercifully, the only car on the road seemed to be ours.

My mother noticed me quivering. “Ike, slow down a little would you? We had an accident a few months ago. Now Korel is scared of cars. She’s shaking.”

Great! Advertise all my fears to the world, Mom. “No. I’m fine. Really I am. I’m just a little cold, that’s all.”

Ike cranked up the heater.

There was a sudden flash.

“Hey, did you see that?” Pete exclaimed. I’ve never seen lightning in the winter before.”

Be quiet! Let Uncle Ike concentrate on the road.

We slowed to a crawl. There was zero visibility. The car suddenly jerked to the right as its front tires slipped into the ditch. I let out an involuntary scream.

“Sorry.” Ike apologized. “Is everybody all right?”

“Yes,” we all said in unison.

Ike and Pete got out to assess the situation.

“She’s not stuck too bad,” my uncle announced. “Angelina, can you drive while we push?”

Mom figured she remembered how. While Ike, Joe and I pushed, she worked the pedals. The car didn’t budge. Uncle Ike and Pete took turns shovelling. Then finally, after half an hour of pushing, shovelling, and pedalling, we worked ourselves free. By that time, the storm had miraculously abated as well. The remainder of the trip to Saskatoon was fairly uneventful.

When we reached the city, I whispered, “Thank you God for sparing us this time.”

“Give me a call if you need me, sis,” Uncle Ike said, stopping in front of Grosma and Bopa’s house. He didn’t come in; it was very late and the lights were off. He gave Mom and me a bear hug. “Take care of that mother of yours, Korel.”

My grandmother, having been informed we were coming, had left the back door unlocked and had put fresh sheets on the double bed in the guest room.

Mom and I, exhausted from our ordeal, went straight to bed.

66

IN BED, MOM snuggled closer to me. When she had been younger she had vowed that when she had children of her own they would never feel unloved as she had.

She loved her mother but felt closer to her father. True, during most of her childhood years he had had a bad temper, but at least he hadn't been cold like her mama. She had often felt that while her papa hit her, it was actually her mama he was mad at, though he would never raise a hand to his wife. As soon as Papa came through the door after a hard day of work, Mama would start complaining to him about the kids, and she, Angelina, had often been the one punished for things the younger ones had done.

Surely Mama had known that if she complained to Papa, he would give her, Angelina, a beating? She must have known! So why then had she done it? The answer, she figured, was obvious—Mama just hadn't cared; she just didn't love her.

Angelina often wondered, did Mama perhaps regret not selling her to that rich farmer and his wife all those years ago? Mama would have been rich, would not have had to work so hard if she had. And what would Angelina's life have been like?

Was it perhaps hope that prompted her to keep coming back home now? Hope that someday her mother would love her?

67

IT WAS MID-MORNING; we had just finished our breakfast when we heard the knock on the door. Mom and I looked at each other, our hearts stopped. Was it him? We stayed in the kitchen, hidden from view, while Bopa went to see who it was.

There stood Joe, unshaven and haggard.

The man must have driven all night, Bopa thought.

"Are Angelina and Korel here?" Joe enquired, quickly scanning the room and beyond.

"Why are you here?" Bopa gruffly asked his son-in-law. "You threatened to kill my daughter and granddaughter."

"No, it wasn't like that. I would never kill them," Joe cried. "Please, let me explain."

"No. No more talk. I've heard enough of your talk. Go from our house now. I don't wish to see you on our doorstep again."

"But, please, sir, just let me talk to Angelina."

"Go. Now!" Abe Bickert, like his son, Ike, may have been

short but he was solid, strong from years of hard work, and he had no intention of listening to any more of this man's excuses.

Joe knew he was not going to get anywhere with my grandfather. He turned around and left.

"Abe, you should have at least given the man a chance to explain himself," Grosma, who had taken in the conversation, whispered. "After all, he drove all night just to see her." To her way of thinking, Joe was family, regardless of how he and her daughter got along. Once family, always family.

"No. He is smart," Bopa argued. "He knows the right words to make her come back to him. That man is smart, too smart. He's so smart, he isn't all home upstairs."

I WAS WASHING dishes for my Grosma while she and my Mom sat talking at the table when the call came asking for a Mrs. Jaslo. It was a nurse from St. Paul's Hospital.

"Your husband is in critical condition," she explained. "He ingested a cleaning fluid."

The nurse in my mother was instantly aroused. "I've got to get over to the hospital right away. Joe drank poison."

Bopa took Grosma aside. "She shouldn't go," he said.

"But, Abe. Of course she has to go. He's her husband."

"He did it just to get her to come back to him."

"For shame, Abe. The man might be dying."

MY GRANDFATHER DROVE my mother to the hospital.

"From what I can gather," the doctor told her, "he had been using carbon tetrachloride to degrease a part in his car. He said that, intending to take a drink of gin, he accidentally swallowed some of the solvent instead."

The doctor might have had his own private doubts about it being accidental, but that was neither here nor there. The main concern right now was keeping Joe alive. Carbon tet was a highly toxic fluid that could cause any one of his vital organs to shut down.

It was Christmas Eve and my mother was spending it sitting beside her husband in the hospital as he slipped in and out of consciousness. It wasn't for love; she would have done as much for an injured dog. She spent the night in the room reserved for family members.

I stayed back with my grandparents. I didn't mind staying with them—I had spent a week with them years earlier in the summer, while they still lived on the farm. I had especially enjoyed spending time with Grosma's hens, picking them up and petting them, searching for eggs or just sitting perched on an overturned bucket in their midst trying to imitate their cackles. Another thing I had liked was Grosma's dill salad. She would pick lettuce and dill fresh from the garden and mix it with mayonnaise, cream, and a little sugar.

Both Grosma and Bopa were good to me, and I was respectful in turn, though I didn't feel particularly close to them. But then there were very few people I really could be myself with anyway. To survive in an adult world, I had adapted to its expectations of me. People were always saying things like, "Korel is so well-behaved." "She's so polite." "Never any trouble." Mom told me that she had always been so proud of me. "Even as a toddler you never touched anyone's ornaments, made a mess at someone's house, or ran around screaming and hollering as some children do. You would always sit so nicely on their couch...the only person who ever found grief with you," Mom told me, "was that horrid cousin of Joe's, Judy. But then she was probably just jealous because her own kids were such brats."

I remembered that. I remembered how bored I had always felt when out visiting with my parents, how I wished I could go back home where I could be me.

Sometimes I'd feel suffocated, as though I couldn't breathe, so I'd go to the bathroom and behind the closed door make the most horrible faces. I'd roll my eyes and stick out my tongue, and wiggle my fingers in my ears. I'd make silent screams and, lifting each leg in turn, silently stomp it on the floor. Then I'd walk out and quietly return to the sofa. I remembered watching shows like *Danger Man*, and *Peter Gunn* on people's sofas. I had memorized the jingle from a commercial too:

Smoke DuMaurier for real smoking pleasure.
DuMaurier, the cigarette of good taste,
a mild cigarette with the best filter yet.
That's why the trend today
is smoke DuMaurier.

Yes, I was being the "good little girl" for my grandparents but I was so happy to see my mother walk through the door Christmas morning! She and I had been through so much together and I worried about her and missed her.

Bopa and Grosma did their best to give Mom and me a good Christmas. There was turkey and there were presents, but for me it just wasn't the same.

That horrid beast had taken up residency inside my stomach again. It came and went in waves. But now it had sprouted an extra head. The one head was the sorrow, the longing, for whom or what, I had no idea; and the other one, the new one, was boredom, restlessness. The two-headed monster cried and crawled around inside my belly, eating me from the inside out.

Relief came only when I slept.

That evening I went to the hospital with Mom.

"You need me right now," I said to her. Could it be that I needed her as well? *No, of course not.*

I went into my father's room. I didn't want to but I felt I should. There he lay with wires poking out everywhere. He didn't look like the fiend I had been envisioning lately; the fiend from the bowels of hell, intent upon our destruction, but his present condition seemed equally ominous. Death stood beside him—Joe was pasty white and his eyes looked hollow.

"Korel," he rasped, reaching out a shaky hand.

I felt like running for my life, this was a scene from a horror movie, but I edged closer and allowed him to take my hand. He squeezed it weakly. I went through the niceties for a few minutes then scooted back to the visitor's room.

Mom had worried about the effect seeing him in that condition would have on me, but I felt no sympathy. The only thing I was concerned about was when Mom and I could leave.

"I want to go home," I told her irritably.

"I know, dear, I do too, but we can't just leave him here, with no one to care. We don't know yet if he's going to make it. His kidneys have shut down."

"Why? Why can't we just go home and let the nurses look after him? Why do we have to stay?"

"Korel," my mother was shocked. "How can you say that? Of course we have to stay. He's sick. He may die."

"Well, you stay with him, then," I retorted. "I want to go home."

Mom couldn't understand it. How could I not feel at least some pity? As I lay in the visitor's room that night I pondered that question myself. I felt guilty about my lack of emotion. *Am I a callous person?* After all, he had always been there for me when *I* was sick. One time he had even burnt out the motor in the car—he had been in the middle of changing the oil—just to get me to the hospital when my heart acted up.

Yes, but this is different.

Why? How is this any different?

I don't know, it just is.

"I don't want him to die, God," I muttered, "I just want him to leave us alone."

68

MOM PHONED MRS. CHIMCO, asking if I could stay there for awhile. She had taken Betty into her confidence before and had come to trust the big-hearted woman.

"Of course," Mrs. Chimco said, "We'd be glad to have Korel. Melanie will be so happy."

Two days after Christmas, I was on the bus back to Lethbridge. My grandparents had paid for my fare. It was at times like this, when people were so good to me, that I felt inadequate. "Thank you," always sounded so hollow, so unappreciative.

Mom was good at thank yous. When she thanked you, you really felt thanked. She would hug you and grasp your hand. Tears would flow out of her eyes and she would go on and on about how thankful she was. But I was unable to do that; it just wasn't in me to get all dramatic and teary-eyed.

It seemed to me, though, that my Grosma understood.

She wasn't much for big hugs and gushy words, either. When I went to board the bus, Grosma squeezed my shoulders then quickly looked away, but not before I caught the sheen in her eyes. Bopa hugged me and slipped something into my hand. It turned out to be a five-dollar bill.

I leaned back and waited for the bus to depart. I enjoyed travelling by bus, especially alone. It was roomy enough that I didn't feel entombed, as I did in a car. On a bus, I was free to let my mind wander, to explore theological thoughts and to follow my quest for the truth. The two-headed beast quickly vacated my being.

I opened the notebook in which I kept and reflected upon my musings. Pen in hand I began to write...

> *The truth—how might one go about obtaining it? Veracity, I believe, is not limited to the Bible; it may be found in many places, if one just looks for it. Obtaining the truth might be compared to a group of people confined to a room, people who, beyond squinting through pin-sized holes on the wall, have never seen the outside world. If each person limited his peeping to only one particular hole, his view would most certainly be distorted. One person, for example, upon spotting soil, may say he has seen the world and it is brown, while another, seeing grass, will swear it's green, and a third, taller person might argue it's blue. To get a more accurate picture, each would have to look through all the vents. So it is with religion. We must not confine ourselves to any one denomination...*

I paused in my writing, my thoughts turning to the myth of Prometheus and Pandora, the Greek legend I had first learned of many years earlier. Touring through the library, I had managed to find more information on them.

I continued with my writing...

> *Prometheus was supposedly a Titan, an immortal giant who gave man the gift of fire. At this, Zeus, king of gods, had grown angry because man would now consider himself equal to the gods. So he had Prometheus bound to a rock where he was tortured daily by an eagle. The Titan, an eternal, could not die—each night his wounds healed. What kept him sane was a secret he knew: that Zeus would one day father a child with a mortal woman. This child, part mortal, part god, would one day free Prometheus. The child's name would be Hercules.*
>
> *It seems to me that this story has parallels to the Bible. The Bible also mentions giants at the beginning of time. The gift of fire finds its parallel in the tree of knowledge. This gift of fire, or tree of knowledge, must obviously then be a symbol for man's intellect. In both cases, God was upset that man gained this intelligence, and someone—Prometheus, the Serpent?—had been punished. Is, perchance, Satan the Bible's counterpart to Prometheus?*
>
> *As in the Greek myth, the Bible states that God the father sired a child—Jesus—with a mortal woman. But the Bible doesn't say that Jesus would one day free the Serpent. Satan therefore, cannot be Prometheus' counterpart. So who is?*

And why would man's newly found intelligence bother God? Why do both stories stress that he had become angry? Was God really a jealous being or was it something else? Could it be that intelligence robbed early man of the innocence of a more animal-like mentality, that it brought upon him Pandora's gifts of misery and guile? If that is the case, intelligence has harmed man and it was that which raised God's wrath.

And what does peep-hole number three—science—have to say on the matter? It claims our ancestors were apes. Therefore it would seem that all three—Greek myth, Bible and science—agree. Man at one time held the innocence and intelligence of an animal. And according to the Greek myth, the Goddess of Innocence will one day return, because hope is the one thing that didn't escape from Pandora's box.

I closed my book of musings. The one thing for which I was thankful to Joe was his stress on the importance of broadening my mind, and questioning accepted norms.

The bus pulled into Medicine Hat. There would be an hour's wait between connections, so I headed to the cafeteria and ordered a ham sandwich with chips. In another few hours, I would be back in Lethbridge.

Would everything still be the same there?

I would be fifteen in three more weeks. When I was younger, in my horse-playing days, I'd daydream that when I turned sixteen my remuda and I, along with like-minded people, would run away to the mountains. We would find shelter in caves and preserve grass in jars for the winter, and when we had children, we would teach them to love animals and the land.

Sixteen, back then, had seemed so far away, but now it was only a year in the future. I no longer planned to live off grass and I was happy in Lethbridge, but I still wished that I could someday teach people to be kind to animals. I liked the Taoist philosophy of living a simple and spontaneous life, like a child, and following the way of nature. It seemed to me that Jesus held similar beliefs—he said that we must be as children to enter the Kingdom of Heaven.

MR. CHIMCO AND Melanie were at the bus terminal when I arrived. They drove me to my house and waited so that I could grab a few more things I needed.

I walked through the door. Everything was the same but not. Though I had been gone just days, it felt like years. The house I had once breathed in, slept in and laughed in, now felt alien—hostile.

I walked from room to room turning on the lights, trying to expel the darkness. I went into the living room, turned on the switch, and then went up to the unlit tree. As I bent down to plug in the string of bulbs, I spotted a present with the words:

To Korel,

Merry Christmas,

Love Daddy.

I backed up, slapped myself—hard—and walked out to the waiting car.

To be continued...

About the Author

Donna Miller has always wanted to write a book but never had the time, having spent a couple of her teen years and most of her adult ones raising six children—not bad for an only child. But no regrets. Her children, grandchildren and greats are her "bestest" friends.

She now spends much of her time writing, and in the summer, working at the Farmers' Market, gardening and tenting. She lives in Rosetown, Saskatchewan.